The Junior Tennis Handbook

Other books by Skip Singleton:

Intelligent Tennis: A Sensible Approach to Playing Your Best Tennis ... Consistently
Intelligent Doubles: A Sensible Approach to Better Doubles Play

The Junior Tennis Handbook

A Complete Guide to Tennis for Juniors, Parents, and Coaches

Skip Singleton

USPTA Master Professional

SHOE TREE PRESS
WHITE HALL, VIRGINIA

Published by Shoe Tree Press, an imprint of
Betterway Publications, Inc.
P.O. Box 219
Crozet, VA 22932
(804) 823-5661

Cover design by Rick Britton and Skip Singleton
Cover artwork by Serigraphia
Photographs by Tim Swanson
Typography by Park Lane Associates

Cataloging-in-Publication Data

Singleton, Skip
    The junior tennis handbook: a complete guide to tennis for juniors,
    parents, and coaches / Skip Singleton.
      p. cm.
    Includes index.
    Summary: A compendium of information about the game of tennis with
    instructions for mastering playing techniques.
    ISBN 1-55870-192-3 : $12.95
    1. Tennis--Handbooks, manuals, etc.--Juvenile literature.
    [1. Tennis.] I. Title.
    GV996.5.S56 1991
    796.342'2--dc20   90-21927
                                         CIP
                                         AC

Printed in the United States of America
0 9 8 7 6 5 4 3 2 1

*This book is dedicated to the two people who have always
supported me and to whom I owe my tennis career . . .
my parents, Anne and Paul Singleton.*

*To my wife, Debbie,
without whom this book could not have been written,
Thank you.*

*And to my Godson, Patrick.
You're already a tennis star in my eyes!*

ACKNOWLEDGMENTS

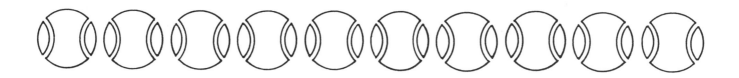

I would like to thank the many fine and talented people who influenced me in a positive way with the sport of tennis when I was a junior: Jim McLennan, Bill Monan, Jack Leonard, Raine Hunt, Peter Burwash, Jeff Gray, Greg Hilley, Peter Scott, Russell Blair, Ben Brown, Larry Anchors, Scott Gilmore, Rae Parrish, Curley Walters & Peter Pizzo.

Thanks for inspiring me with this great game in the early years of my life. Your encouragement and belief helped to shape the positive feelings I still have today for the game of tennis . . . and will have for the rest of my life!

CONTENTS

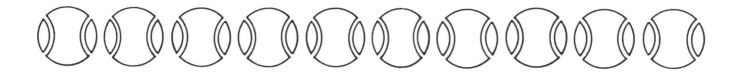

Chapter 1

UNDERSTANDING THE GAME

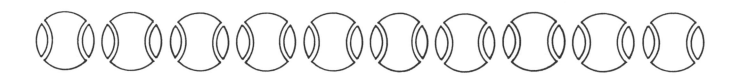

THE ORIGINAL GAME OF TENNIS

The game of tennis, as we know it today, is really a newer version of the old game of "real" or "royal" tennis that has been played for many hundreds of years indoors.

Tennis was originally called "Sphairistike" when it was invented by Major Walter Clopton Wingfield in 1873. The game was played throughout England on grass lawns with an hourglass-shaped court. This later became known as "lawn tennis." Thanks largely to another lawn tennis pioneer, Major Harry Gem, the court eventually took on its rectangular shape.

It was Wimbledon, the first tennis tournament in the world, that transformed a social game into a major international sport. The tournament committee, composed of Henry Jones, Julian Marshall, and C.G. Heathcote, devised the rules of the game that have held — except for minor changes — ever since. Serving underhanded and charging the net, Spencer W. Gore was the sport's first champion, winning Wimbledon 6-1, 6-2, 6-4 over W. Marshall in 1877. In 1884 a women's singles event was played at Wimbledon for the first time and was won by Maud Watson, who defeated her sister Lilian in the finals.

In 1881, several years after tennis came to the United States from England, a small group of tennis enthusiasts formed the United States National Lawn Tennis Association. Their purpose was to standardize the rules of the game and to develop the sport of tennis in this country. The first tennis championship of the U.S. was held in Newport, Rhode Island, where the International Tennis Hall of Fame is now located. The first winner was R.D. Sears, who successfully defended his title six consecutive times — an accomplishment that has never been repeated. The first women's championship in the United States was held in 1887 in Philadelphia at the Cricket Club and was won by Ellen Hansell.

THE COURT

Court surfaces have changed over the years from the traditional grass court surface to easier-to-maintain surfaces like hard, clay, or synthetic surface courts. They can be found indoors as well as outdoors.

Grass. Grass courts require constant upkeep and maintenance to remain in top condition. Wimbledon is the only major tennis championship that is still played on grass. Balls tend to "skip" or "slide" on this surface, making grass courts one of the fastest playing surfaces in the world.

Grass

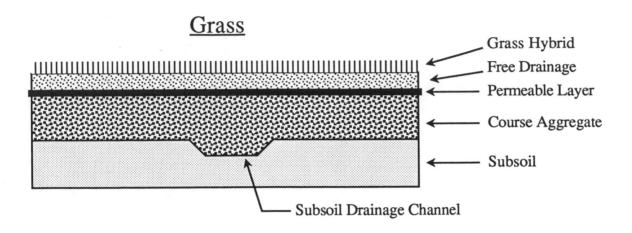

- Grass Hybrid
- Free Drainage
- Permeable Layer
- Course Aggregate
- Subsoil

Subsoil Drainage Channel

Hard

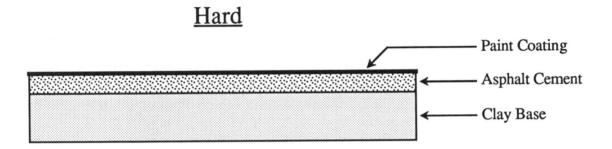

- Paint Coating
- Asphalt Cement
- Clay Base

Clay & Synthetic Clay

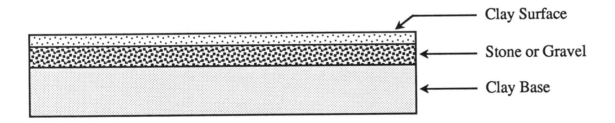

- Clay Surface
- Stone or Gravel
- Clay Base

Synthetic Grass

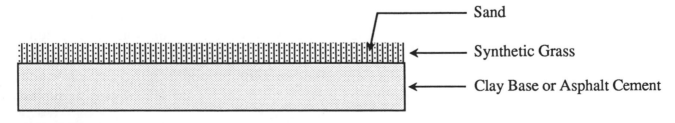

- Sand
- Synthetic Grass
- Clay Base or Asphalt Cement

Court surfaces.

Hard. Very little maintenance is needed for hard surface courts. It is the most popular surface in the U.S. and the surface used at the U.S. Open Championships. The surface offers a "true" bounce for the all-court player and generally plays faster than clay courts.

Clay and Synthetic Clay. Clay courts need regular maintenance including watering, sweeping, and rolling. They are extremely popular in the U.S. and all over the world. The slower play on the clay court is more suited for the backcourt player and the older set who enjoy the softer and cooler feel of the court under their feet.

Synthetic. There is a variety of synthetic surfaces on the market and most of them are easy to maintain. Play-ability varies from surface to surface. Synthetic grass (as shown) offers the soft feel of grass and the play-ability of clay, with very little maintenance.

THE RULES OF THE GAME

The tennis court is bounded by lines (generally white in color). Any ball that touches the boundary line, or lands within the court area bound by it, is deemed "good," or playable. A ball hit outside the playing area is called "out," but only after it bounces.

The backline on either side of the net is called the *baseline*; the line running parallel to the baseline and the net is called the *serviceline*; the center line that runs perpendicular to the net and the serviceline is called the *center serviceline*; the outside lines that connect the baseline with the net are called the *doubles sidelines*; the lines that run parallel to the doubles sidelines are the *singles sidelines*. The court area between the singles and doubles sidelines is known as the *doubles alley*. The game of singles is played within the area bounded by the singles sidelines, while doubles is played in the entire court area.

The Game of Singles

Singles is played with two players standing on opposite sides of the net; the player who first strikes the ball is the *server*, while the player who returns it is called the *receiver*. A toss of a coin or the spin of a racket decides who will be the first server. The player winning the toss may choose, or require his opponent to choose: a) the right to be server or receiver, giving the other player the choice of side; b) the side, the other player choosing to serve or receive; or c) giving the other person the first choice.

The server stands behind the baseline on the right side of the court, within the imaginary continuations of the center mark and the singles sideline. Serves are directed diagonally across the net into the left service box by throwing the ball up into the air and striking it with the racket before it drops to the ground. If the ball does not fall into the service box, it is called a *fault*. A second serve is then allowed. If the second serve does not fall into the proper service court, it is termed a *double fault* and the server loses the point. If the serve, however, lands good in the appropriate box, the receiver returns the ball into the singles court across the net and the point continues. Now the point will be decided either by an error (when one player either hits the ball into the net, hits it out of the playing area, or misses it entirely) or by a winner (when one player hits into the playing area a ball that is not returnable by the opponent). The ball is allowed only one bounce on each side of the net before it must be returned, or a loss of the point results.

Servers alternate their service deliveries to the left and right service boxes after each point has been played. If the service ball touches the net but lands in the correct box, it is called a *let*

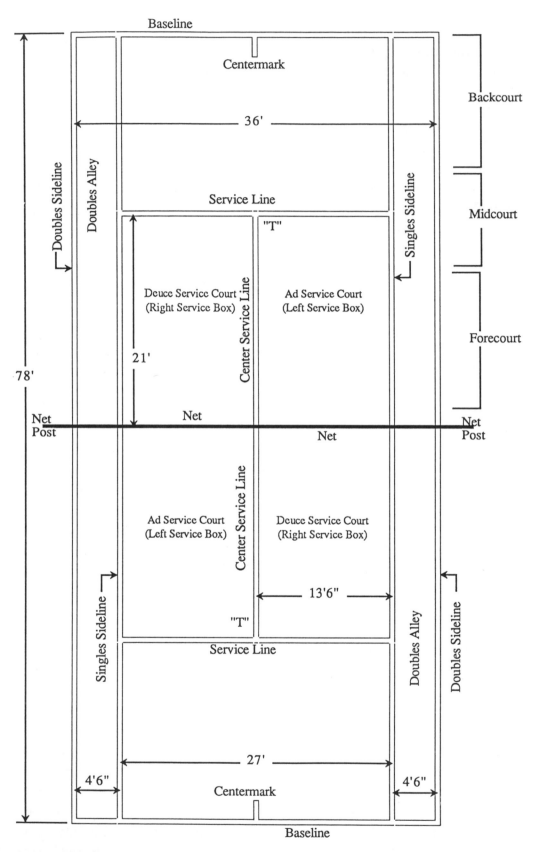

A Court layout.

and the serve is replayed. If the ball touches the net but does not land in the service box it is a fault. The only time the ball must be allowed to bounce before the player returns it is on the service. Thereafter, the receiver is allowed to hit the ball either before or after the first bounce.

At the conclusion of each game, service duties alternate from player to player. Players change sides after the first game and every following odd numbered game in each set.

The Game of Doubles

In doubles, there are two players on each side of the net. Each team must decide who will serve first for the pair and who will return from each side at the service court. The order of receiving and serving shall not be altered during the set but may be changed at the beginning of each new set that is played.

The rules of doubles are quite the same as they are in singles except that the boundary lines are the farthest lines that bound the court in doubles, thus enlarging the playing area.

SCORING

There are four or more points in a game and six or more games in a set. The points in a game are called *15*, *30*, *40*, and *game*, which is the equivalent of 1, 2, 3, and 4 points. Players must win a game by at least a two point margin, so if the score reaches 40-40 (or 40 all), it is called *deuce*. A player now has to win two points in succession to win the game. The first point following deuce is called *advantage*, or "ad" to the person winning the point. If this player does not win the next point the score returns to deuce.

Whenever the score is announced, the server's score is given before the receiver's. If the server is leading by three points to one, the score is called "40-15." Zero (or no points) is called "love" in tennis. If the server is leading by one point to none, for example, the score is called "15-love." If the server has won one point but lost two, the score is called "15-30."

The serve is alternated in every game with each player serving the game in its entirety. The player who first wins six games — with a margin of two games — wins the set. A player can win a set by scores of 6-0, 6-1, 6-2, 6-3, 6-4, but 6-5 is not a completed set score since there is less than a margin of two games separating the players. 7-5 would be the score to complete the set. If the players reach 6-6 (six games all), a *tie-breaker* is played to determine the winner.

Most matches are the best of three tie-break sets. The first player to win two sets wins the match. If each player wins a set, a third set is then played to decide the winner. In major international championships, the men (not the women) often play best of five set matches, which requires the winner to win three sets to claim victory in each match.

The Tie-Break

When the score reaches six games all, a tie-break is used to determine a winner for the set. The first player to win seven points wins the set as long as there is at least a two point margin in the score. Numerical scoring is used throughout the tie-break. If the score reaches six points all, the tie-break is extended until a margin of two points separates the players.

The player whose turn it is to serve is the server for the first point. Only one point is served by the first player and thereafter, each player serves alternately for two consecutive points until the winner of the set is decided. The first service point begins from the right court and every service alternates court sides thereafter. The second server serves the second and third points from the left and right courts respectively; the next serves for the fourth and fifth points from the left and right courts; and so on. Players change sides of the court each time six points have been played until a winner has emerged.

SPORTSMANSHIP AND THE CODE OF CONDUCT

In tennis, players show respect and consideration for not only their partners and opponents but also for players on adjacent courts. It is important that common courtesy be extended to all persons on and around the courts by the players involved in the game:

1. Enter and exit the court between points if someone is playing on an adjacent court.

2. Don't talk to players while they are engaged in a point or involved in a match. Always keep your voice down around the courts when people are playing.

3. Return all balls to adjoining courts as soon as possible, but only when there is a break in the points they are playing.

4. When your opponent is serving and the point is over, gently return all balls on your side of the court directly to the server.

5. If your opponent serves a fault, do not go after or return the ball. Wait until after the second serve has been played so you won't interrupt and disturb the server's timing (unless the ball is lying in your playing area).

6. 50% of all players involved in tennis matches will lose — accept defeat graciously and without offering excuses. Avoid getting angry at yourself or your opponent and above all, avoid arguments of any kind.

7. You are to call all balls on your side of the net. If you do not clearly see a ball and are unable to make a call, you can either ask your opponent to help you on the call or you must

award the point to your opponent. Never call a ball on your opponent's side of the net unless your help is solicited. Do not enlist the help of spectators.

8. If a ball has touched even a portion of the line, it is good. Give opponents the benefit of the doubt on all calls, no matter the score.

9. When moving around the court, do not wave your racket or arms or otherwise attempt to distract your opponent during play.

10. As the server, call the score regularly. If there is a disagreement on the score, go back to the last score that you are both in agreement on.

11. Calls of "out" or "let" should be made instantly.

12. Play is to be continuous. Toweling off, drinking, etc. are permitted only at game changeovers and should not exceed ninety seconds.

13. Coaching or any other interference is prohibited during match-play.

14. Be familiar with and follow the rules of the game.

15. Following matches that you play, always shake hands with your opponents.

CHOOSING THE RIGHT EQUIPMENT

Rackets
When choosing your equipment, your racket purchase will likely be your most costly initial expense. If a quality racket is selected, however, it should last for years.

Rackets come in a variety of head and body sizes, lengths, stiffnesses, grip sizes, and weights, not to mention colorful designs and styles. Until early 1970 almost every player who had won a tennis title had done it with a wooden racket. Today it's difficult to find any racket companies producing wooden frames since materials such as graphite, fiberglass,

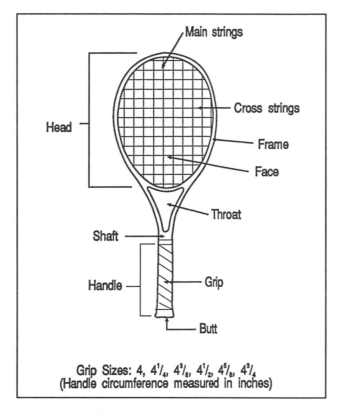

Parts of a racket.

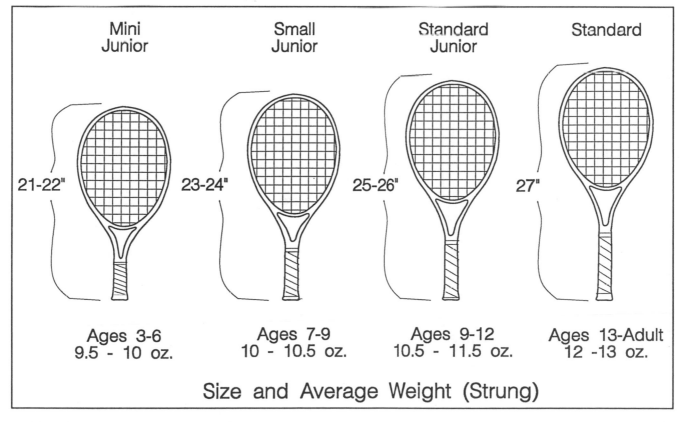

There are different sizes of rackets.

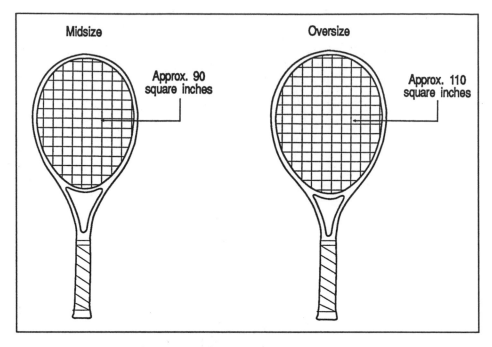

There are also two sizes of racket heads.

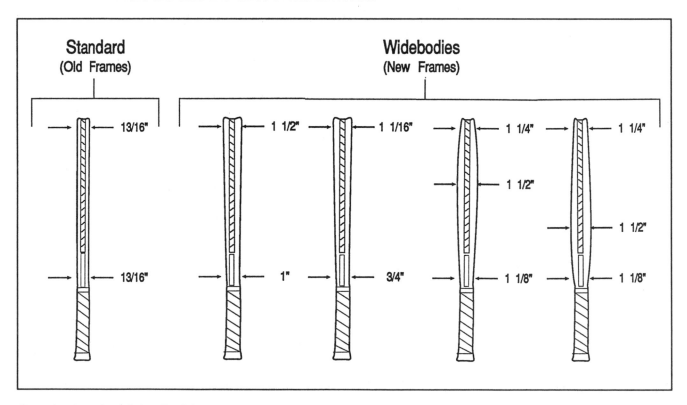

Standard and widebodied frames.

metal, aluminum, boron, or composite are the choice of today's players.

The best way to select your racket is to demonstrate or "test" several rackets from your local tennis shop. Every racket has different and unique playing characteristics and you should make certain that the racket you choose is the one that feels right for you. Seek the qualified help of the professional or shop manager in making your racket decision. Check to make sure that the weight, balance, and grip are suitable to your own size and that you are choosing the correct frame for your age and level of play.

Most rackets are sold as "frames only," which means they come unstrung. There are almost as many different strings available on the market today as there are rackets. They come in all different gauges, colors, materials, and textures.

Gut strings used to be what rackets were strung with in the early days of tennis, and they still remain the top choice of professionals and tennis enthusiasts today. Although considered by many to be the "best" string available, gut does have its share of drawbacks. It is not only the most expensive string sold, it isn't even considered a very durable or long lasting one. So why is gut still preferred? Feeling—the resiliency, liveliness, and feel of gut remains unsurpassed!

String manufacturers have come out over the years with a wide variety of nylon and synthetic gut strings that are much more affordable, are longer lasting, and offer very close playing characteristics to that of natural gut. By doing so, these synthetic strings have (by far) become more popular with players at all levels. Consult your local tennis shop about which strings they would recommend for your new racket. They will probably have a variety of nylon and synthetic gut strings that will not only look good in your racket but will also per-

form at a price you'll find affordable.

Every racket has a recommended tension by the manufacturer and should be strung accordingly. Again, your local qualified professional or certified racket stringer can help you select the correct pounds of tension to have your racket strung at. As a rule of thumb, *higher*, or tighter, tensions provide control but reduce power, wear the strings more quickly, and shorten the life of the frame. *Lower* tensions provide more power, are easier on the arm, and lengthen the life of the strings and frame.

Balls

In the long run, tennis balls may be your greatest expense in playing this game since they will need to be constantly replaced. Old, used, and worn-out tennis balls that have little bounce or "fuzz" on their surface shouldn't be used for match-play, but make excellent balls to practice with (serving, for example). Depending on your level of play, three to six sets of tennis are the useful life of most balls.

Officially tested and approved tennis balls are the only ones you should purchase. Most of them come in pressure sealed plastic cans, which you can feel before purchasing to insure premium quality. "Extra duty felt" balls are better suited for long-lasting play on hard court surfaces, while "regular felt" balls are best for clay and synthetic court surfaces.

Clothing and Shoes

Clothing should be comfortable to allow for free and easy movement. Although once "white only" tennis attire was acceptable, today few clubs and tennis facilities still list this as a requirement for play. While some clubs do require players to wear collared shirts, t-shirts and most shorts are perfectly acceptable at many others.

Players should dress comfortably while playing the game. Most clubs and tennis facilities have relaxed dress codes and will allow T-shirts and bright colors.

It is recommended that socks be thick enough to absorb perspiration and provide extra cushion. Many players (including myself) opt for double protection by wearing two pairs of socks while playing the game.

Like rackets and strings there are a number of shoes available on the market for tennis play. Look for items such as arch support, heel cushion and protection, and durable soles when making your purchase. The shoes you choose should be comfortable and correctly sized. They should also have a sole that is suited to the court surface you will be playing on most often.

Accessories

Go into any tennis shop and you will likely find a large number of tennis accessories. Wristbands, headbands, overgrips, replacement grips, shock absorption devices, head protection tape, sawdust or grip enhancement powders, elbow, wrist and knee supports are among the many others. Most of these items are quite useful; however, many of them remain little more than "bells and whistles" to your tennis equipment. Consult the professional or shop manager for advice on any of the above mentioned items.

WHEN TO BEGIN

When is the best age to learn to play the game? I've been asked this question many times and my answer is always "whenever they show the interest in the sport."

Jimmy Connors swung his first racket on the court at age two and Chris Evert began her illustrious tennis career at age three. Since

What is the best age to learn to play the game?
As long as tennis remains fun, any age is fine.

each child is unique, so is the decision on when to start them playing the game. Just because these two tennis greats got an early start in the sport doesn't make that the right choice for everyone. I, myself, began playing the game of tennis at the ripe old age of thirteen. Up until that time I had competed in a variety of mostly team sports. Physical and mental maturity levels vary from child to child and certainly play a big role in determining the child's readiness to play the game.

Kids who start early usually don't get turned "off" by tennis, but by parents and coaches who push them too hard and take the fun out of the game! Learning the game at three or four is perfectly all right as long as tennis remains FUN for them. Let their competitiveness surface "naturally" by the enthusiasm they show for the sport and their own willingness and desire to achieve success.

Test their interest in the sport by hitting a few balls on the court with them at an early age. Have them come with you to the tennis club and watch their reaction to the game. Watch a tennis match on television with them or attend a local professional event if possible. Explain how the game is played along with an understanding of the strokes. Watch their reaction to this exposure to the game and remember to judge the interest level on that of the child and not that of your own!

No matter the age of the child, if they aren't interested in going out on the court, they aren't ready to learn to play the game. They should never be forced or pressured into playing. Tennis should begin as a fun exercise and if the interest develops . . . they will have a fun sport that will last them a lifetime.

The United States Tennis Association has begun a "Short Tennis" program patterned after several successful tennis programs for youngsters in other countries, namely Sweden and throughout Europe. Their emphasis has been that "people enjoy what they are good at,"

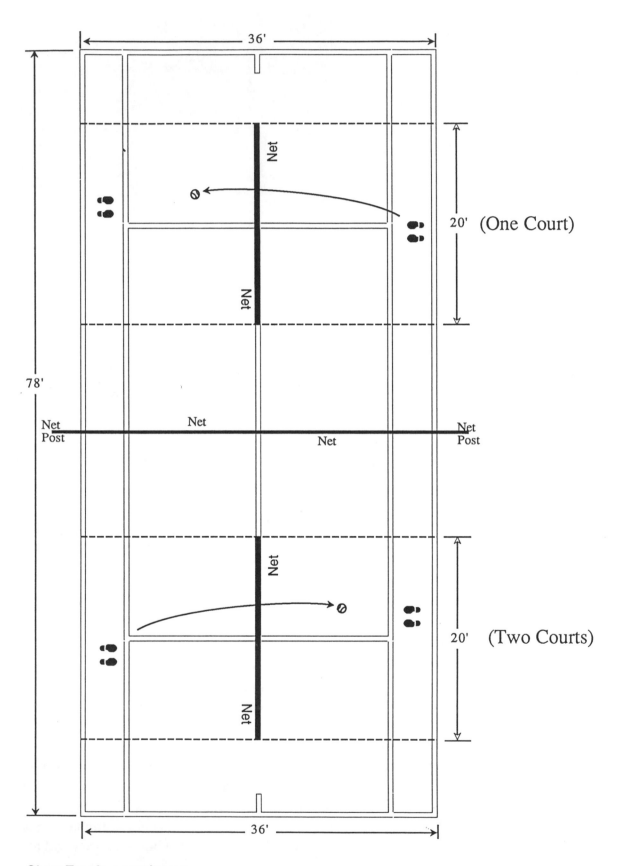

Short Tennis court layout.

and they feel that if more kids experienced longer rallies during their first exposure to the sport they would achieve more satisfaction with the game and desire to continue playing it.

Other sports have been modified for younger children. Basketball hoops are lowered for young athletes while soccer and baseball fields have been scaled down for little competitors. The rules are sometimes even changed for youth sports. T-Ball baseball and touch or flag football, for example, are designed to make the sports easier and more enjoyable for the young participants and have proven quite successful in doing so.

Short Tennis is played on a court approximately 20 feet by 40 feet, using smaller rackets (18-25 inches compared to the standard 27 inches), balls made of foam or dead, low compression ones, and a net that measures 28 inches high instead of the usual 36 inches.

Short Tennis is designed for very young children or for the young beginner who would like to learn to play the game almost immediately. The skills and strategies of tennis are quite the same on the short court, and it has been proven that the transition to a "full size" game of tennis has been an easy one for these young, developing players. For more information, contact: USTA Short Tennis, 707 Alexander Road, Princeton, NJ 08540 for free materials.

SUMMARY

The game of tennis as we know it today has been around just over a century. It was first called "lawn tennis" and played on grass tennis courts throughout England. Hard, clay, and synthetic surface courts have mostly replaced grass as the surface of choice; however, the Wimbledon Tennis Championship — the premier tennis tournament in the world — is still played on grass courts.

It is important to learn the rules of the game as well as how to keep score before playing. Remember, always be courteous and sportsmanlike on and around the courts. When choosing your equipment seek the help of a qualified professional or shop manager at a local tennis shop. They can give good advice on racket selections as well as stringing suggestions. Demo or test several rackets before making your purchase to insure lasting satisfaction.

Check the club or tennis facility you will be playing at before purchasing clothing, shoes, or balls. There may be a dress code for players, and the surface type will determine which shoes and balls will be best suited.

Kids are ready to begin playing tennis once they've shown an interest in the game. Parents can expose their children to the sport, but the child's interest level will ultimately determine his or her state of readiness to begin learning the game.

Chapter 2

LEARNING THE STROKES

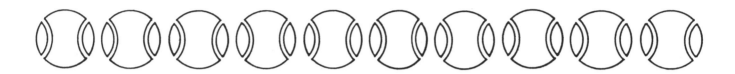

THE READY POSITION

Tennis players prepare for the ball to be directed their way by assuming the "ready position." When in the ready position, players are better poised to spring into action for their shots, much like a sprinter who is waiting for the sound of the gun.

To stand correctly in the ready position, feet should be spread (roughly) shoulder distance apart with knees slightly flexed. Your upper body should be bent slightly forward with the weight on the balls of your feet. The racket will be loosely held in your hand while your non-dominant hand holds the racket at the throat to support its weight and offer maneuverability.

Establishing good habits in tennis begins with the ready position. Watch the top players in the game. Every one of them has learned to use this basic starting position for initial stroke preparation. Their minds are alert and eyes keenly focused on the ball. Their bodies are ready for immediate action the moment the ball leaves the opponent's racket. This is how world class players make the game look so easy. They are quick off the mark of their opponent's hits and prepare themselves early in the proper position to strike the ball comfortably.

Often the difference between good and great players is what takes place *before* and *after* the shots of the players, not necessarily the strokes of the players themselves. Players who are slow to get into action with their bodies will have difficulty trying to align for the hit and will often err in the process. Those who delay in returning to the ready position following their strokes will also find difficulty in reaching future balls directed their way.

Players normally assume the ready position just behind the baseline in the center of the court. However, net players prepare for the ball in a position much closer to the net, while receivers wait to return a serve from a ready position much closer to the sideline. The ready position is the beginning stance for all shots in tennis (except for the serve) and therefore, is the position to be assumed before each stroke and after each stroke (when there is sufficient time), no matter where you are located on the court.

THE FOREHAND

The forehand stroke can be broken down into four parts: 1. grip, 2. backswing, 3. contact, and 4. follow-through.

The ready position.

Grip

The grip, or hold, of the racket is essential to allow for a vertical racket face at contact. It is important to note, however, that a grip does little more than hold the racket in the required position to direct the ball. The pros use a variety of grips, but each strikes the ball similarly with the racket face vertical at contact.

There are several correct and acceptable forehand grips; each has its strengths and limitations. Many tennis gurus tout one grip over another and demand that all of their students use one particular grip for developing their forehands. I, myself, don't teach one method; I teach individuals, and each person must be evaluated to determine which grip is best suited to his or her game and style of play.

The four basic forehand grips are the *Eastern*, *Continental*, *Western*, and the *Semi-Western*.

Eastern. The Eastern forehand grip is probably the most fundamentally sound of the forehand grips. With this grip, the palm of the hand is directly aligned to direct the racket head and the ball in the same direction. Control of the ball begins with control of the racket head. With the Eastern grip, the palm of the hand and the racket head are able to "work as one," thus allowing players to direct the ball comfortably with their palms on forehand hits.

The best way to find the grip is to place your hand (palm flat) on the strings of your racket face and run your hand down the shaft of the racket until you reach the grip. Now, close your hand, and you are holding your

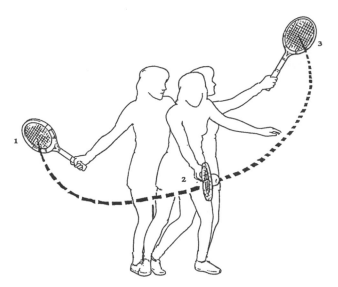

In the forehand stroke, the player takes her racket back (1), allowing for proper contact (2), and then lifts the ball "up" with a correct follow-through of the stroke (3).

racket in an Eastern forehand grip. To check to make sure that the grip is correct, swing the racket out away from your body, then stop (or freeze) to note: 1. If the racket face is vertical, and 2. If the racket face and palm of the hand are aligned with each other. If so, you have the correct grip. If not, repeat the above process of running your hand down the racket until you are able to find the correct Eastern forehand grip.

One of the limitations of the Eastern grip is that it will require grip changes with forehand to backhand hits, as well as with other strokes. Beginners of the game may have difficulty in having enough time to make these grip changes from stroke to stroke. However, it has been proven that even at the highest professional level there is sufficient time to change grips.

Continental. The Continental forehand grip is known as the "versatile grip" in tennis since it can be used for all shots in the game. The Continental grip lies midway between the Eastern forehand and Eastern backhand grip. From the Eastern forehand grip, rotate your hand inward a quarter-turn so that the "V" from your forefinger and thumb lies on the top bevel of the grip handle. With this grip, the wrist must be adjusted to allow for the desired vertical racket head at impact since the palm of the hand will be positioned slightly downward.

Although beginning players may prefer the Continental grip to avoid changing grips on their hits, it is actually a more difficult grip to master. Players must adjust their wrists and then lock them into place for correct forehand hits, which is not an easy task for younger or weaker players. A stronger arm and wrist is required, not to mention talent and coordination, by those choosing to use the Continental grip for forehands. All-court players, who are talented with good feel for the ball along with having a wide variety of hits, are best suited to use the Continental grip. Lower bouncing balls are easily played with this grip, while higher ones become a more difficult task.

Western. The Western forehand grip is achieved by rotating your hand away from the Eastern forehand grip until the palm rests under the grip handle. This extreme forehand grip is commonly used by big topspin hitters and players on slow, clay courts where the ball often bounces very high. Players using Western forehand grips find limitations in low bouncing balls and in the flexibility to play a variety of hits off the forehand side.

Semi-Western. The grip of choice for many of today's professionals and rising stars, the

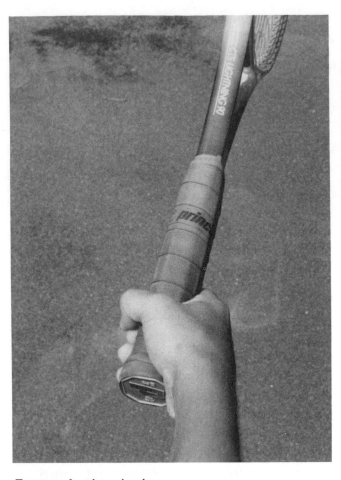
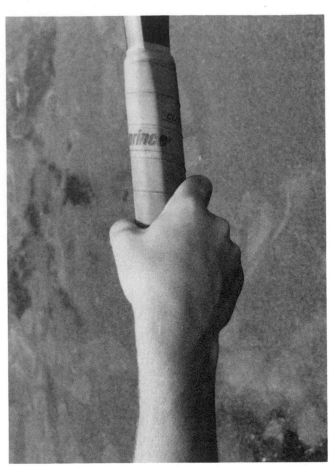

Eastern forehand grip.

Semi-Western provides more of the stability of the Eastern grip along with the ease of topspin of the Western. This grip can be attained by rotating the hand from the Western midway back towards the Eastern. The palm of the hand will rest on the lower outside bevel of the grip handle to provide more "drive" on the swing, much like the Eastern. Lower bouncing balls still remain a problem with this grip. However, forehands hit with Semi-Western grips are more flexible and thus easier to adapt to varying situations on court. The Semi-Western is also ideally suited to control powerful hits best by using natural topspin.

Backswing

Forehand backswings generally come in two forms — the *straight back* and the *loop*. Each is important to understand as well as to be able to execute for successful forehands.

The straight back forehand backswing is the quickest and surest means of preparing the racket to make contact with the ball. The racket is not actually taken straight back at shoulder height; it is really brought back lowered to allow for the "low-to-high swing" of a correct forehand that clears the net and lands within the boundary lines on the opposing side of the court.

It is important to note that a backswing is only for stroke *preparation* and *power*. Some forehand strokes will require little preparation (i.e., hard hit balls or balls directed to you) and some forehand hits will require little power (i.e., softer played shots or when you are posi-

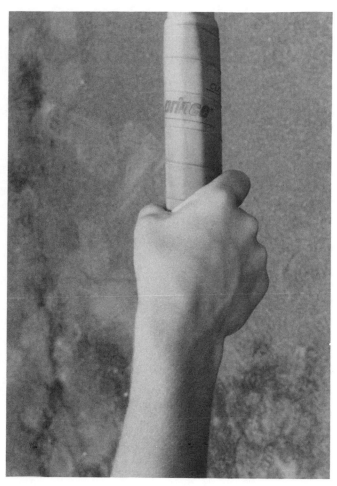

Continental forehand grip.

tioned closer to the net). Other forehands might require more power or preparation, and this is when the backswing becomes a more important factor. Thus, for consistently successful forehand hits, adjustments will need to be made to backswings according to *the shots you are about to play* and according to *the shots played to you.*

The *loop backswing* is the favored choice of the game's most successful competitors. The racket is taken back above or even the height of the oncoming ball and then lowered (thus creating the looping pattern) to come from under the ball to "lift" it over the net. The rhythm of this backswing is preferred by most, and the power that can be generated off the forehand side is that much more enhanced

when the looping backswing is practiced.

You should become familiar with both the loop and the straight back since there will be times when both will have to used while playing. When there is sufficient time, however, the loop should be your choice on the forehand side.

Contact

Contact occurs when the racket face (strings of the racket) and the ball meet with one another. It is important that the racket face be at the proper angle to direct the ball to its desired target. The most essential element in the forehand stroke is the contact, since it is here that control of the ball takes place. One of the most

 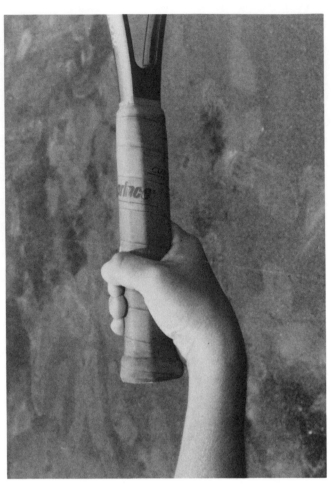

Western forehand grip.

misunderstood basics of the game is that "the ball goes wherever the racket face angle directs it at contact."

The ball actually remains on the strings for only an instant; this is why the racket must be properly aligned in the desired angle to direct the forehand hit with control. A firm grip and wrist help to keep the racket head stable at impact for minimal deflection (racket head movement at impact).

For a reference point, ideal forehand contacts occur in front of the lead foot knee at a comfortable distance away from the body, and at approximately waist high. This early contact with the ball is a good habit to develop for learning optimum control of the ball.

Follow-Through

It has been proven by a number of experts that the follow-through is inconsequential to the stroking process since the ball has already left the racket at contact. The follow-through of the forehand stroke, however, remains important to allow for a greater margin for error at impact by lengthening the contact. Let me explain . . .

Once the racket face makes contact with the ball, the racket should continue moving through the ball in the direction of the desired target. To give a clearer meaning of the follow-through of the forehand, it means to *follow through the ball* on the hit. The longer swing of the ball offers a "guiding" effect, thus giving

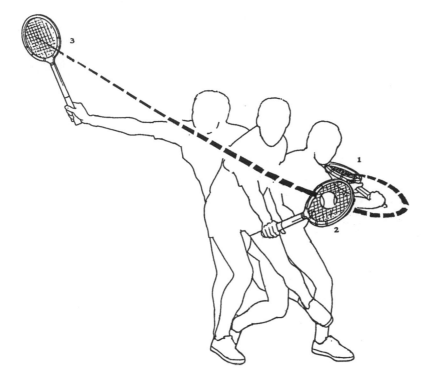

In the backhand stroke, the player has taken his racket into the backswing position (1), and swings forward for a proper contact out in front of the body (2). The racket then continues swinging straight through the ball, lifting it to allow for good net clearance on the shot (3).

better control with the placement of the shot.

The "seven-ball method" will help you to visualize what path the racket needs to take to achieve optimum control on forehand hits. Line up seven balls one behind the other in a straight line on the court. Position yourself behind this line of balls and simulate your forehand stroke over the seven balls. The first ball represents where the contact will take place. Stop your racket at the imaginary contact the first few times to check that the racket face is in the desired angle to direct the ball properly. Continue your swing, keeping the racket face at the same angle to guide the ball to your target. Count all seven balls during your practice swing. It will help you better understand the desired follow-through for ideal forehand hits.

THE BACKHAND

Like the forehand, the backhand stroke has the same four components: the grip, the backswing, contact, and follow-through. The stroke is, however, played on the opposite side of the body and with the reverse face of the racket.

Although both the forehand and the backhand have similar stroking patterns, the backhand is generally the feared stroke to beginners of the game. This is because the ball is taken on the non-dominant side and without the stability offered by the palm on forehand hits.

Grip

The grip for the backhand stroke is less complicated than the forehand grip since there are fewer options in holding the handle on this side. The two preferred backhand grips are the Eastern and the Continental.

Eastern. The Eastern backhand grip is obtained by rotating the hand inwards towards the body until the palm of the hand rests on top of the handle. A good reference point is that the top knuckle of the index finger should be resting on the top handle of the racket.

With this grip, the thumb wraps around

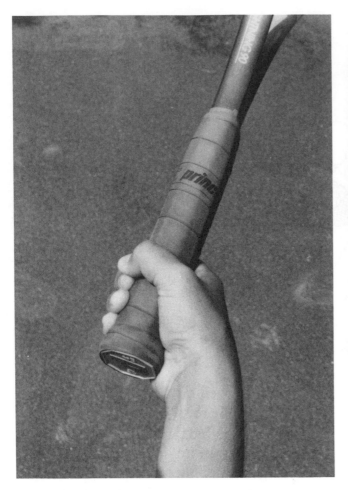 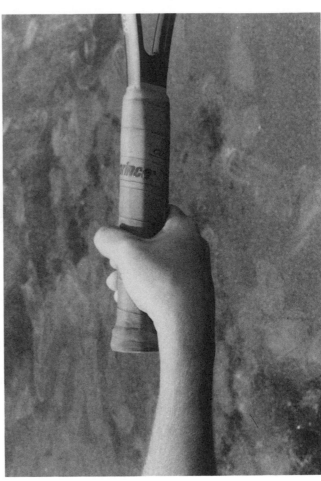

Semi-western forehand grip.

the back of the handle and provides stability at impact. One of the difficulties with backhand hits is usually the lack of *stability*. On forehands, the palm of the hand and entire arm and body are behind the ball at contact, providing force and extra power. On the backhand side, only the thumb is positioned behind the racket.

While the palm guides and directs the ball on forehands, the thumb guides for backhand hits. The top knuckle of the index finger is another reference to use to swing in unison with the racket face towards a target for control.

Continental. The Continental backhand grip is the same grip used for the Continental forehand stroke. That is the beauty of this grip; it requires no grip changes during play (other than wrist adjustment).

While the Eastern grip provides little stability on backhand hits, it still allows more than the Continental. With the Eastern, the entire thumb is behind the racket. Only a portion of the thumb rests behind the racket with the Continental grip. For players with strong wrists and grips, this is enough. However, for many younger and smaller children the strength needed for Continental backhand grips requires that they use the Eastern when learning the backhand stroke.

Backswing

The backswing on the backhand, like the forehand, can be either straight back or a loop. The

The player on the left is demonstrating a correct straight-back backswing, while the player on the right has taken the racket back too high to allow for a correct low-to-high swing.

loop is again preferred for better rhythm and power when time allows.

Each of these backswings should occur with an extended arm (straightened, but not locked). The tendency with many players in the game is to bend the arm at the elbow when drawing the racket back, thus leading into the shot with the elbow first. This causes the ball to often "pop-up" high into the air, since at contact the racket face tilts towards the sky when the racket swings forward.

A quick, early prepared backswing is desired for proper hits out in front of the body. Players who bring their racket back too short and lack power on backhand hits should learn to show the butt end of their racket to the ball at the start of their backhand. By lining your racket up in this manner, not only will more power come to your hits, but control will improve as well since your racket is being prepared in a straight line. The racket is drawn ready to swing directly through the ball on an intended path to a target and in a controlled straight line.

A key to good backswings on the backhand side is the importance of the non-dominant hand. It cradles the racket throat and

draws the racket back, cocked and ready to fire. By using the other hand to help prepare the racket you achieve several things: 1. you will pivot and turn your body sideways to align properly for hits; 2. you will have a guide hand to help the mind visualize where the racket is positioned behind the body; 3. you will place the racket in the desired backswing location with consistency.

Contact

The big difference between contact with the ball in forehand and backhand strokes is that the ball must be contacted farther out in front of the body on backhand hits. The ball should still be met at a comfortable distance away from the body in front of the lead foot knee, and (ideally) waist-high.

The racket face should be vertical at contact (like the forehand) but for this to occur, you must prepare to play the ball an additional *8 to 18 inches* out in front of the body on backhands. The reason lies with the position of your arm. On forehand hits, your dominant arm is farthest away from the ball, while on backhand hits your dominant arm is closest to

A correct loop backswing: the ready position.

Pivot the body.

Drop the racket back.

Come under the ball.

Make contact with the ball.

This player is demonstrating a proper stroke follow-through. By swinging through seven balls she is able to achieve optimum control on her hits.

the ball. By having your arm closer to the ball, out in front of your body, contact with the ball must also occur out farther.

This is the number one most misunderstood basic problem with many backhand hits. Weak, uncontrollable backhand shots could be greatly improved by simply learning to contact the ball farther out in front. Early contact requires early preparation, so quicken your footwork and shorten your backswings for better backhand hits.

Follow-Through

The seven-ball method of visualizing a proper follow-through works well for the backhand

just as it does for the forehand. Throughout this long contact with the ball, keep your head and body stabilized and balanced while your eyes focus on the impact of the ball. The racket will travel through the ball while the arm swings towards the intended target.

The Two-Handed Backhand

Sometimes the easiest way to learn a classic backhand is to simply use two hands on the hit. By using both hands, players are often able to correct one hand stroke deficiencies, not to mention adding power and control to their backhand side.

The two-handed backhand is achieved by

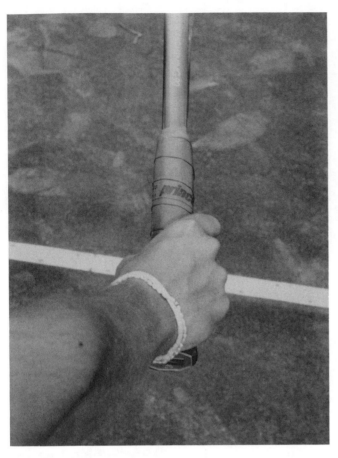 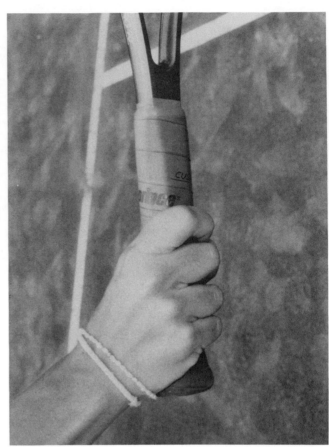

Eastern backhand grip.

placing the non-dominant hand on the handle using an Eastern or a Continental forehand grip, while the regular stroking hand holds the racket with a Continental or an Eastern backhand grip. With the two-handed backhand, the non-dominant grip is even more important, since it will be with this hand that the stroke is driven.

The best way to envision a proper two-handed backhand stroke is to let the racket out of your normal hand and swing a forehand using the weaker arm only. This feels very odd for most but it is important to learn to use this weaker arm for the hit (not just lightly gripping the racket to offer a subtle guide effect). I tell my students that "90% of the swing will come from the other arm on the two-handed shots, so grip firmly and drive through the ball as if you were playing a forehand from your oppo-

site side."

Not only will your other arm play a significant part on your two-handed hit, but your body will also become more involved. Hips pivot more, as do the shoulders, when the stroke is well-executed. This enhances the power on the stroke as the body's chain reaction torques its way through the hit while pivoting into the shot. The second hand on the racket handle also provides added assurance by keeping the racket head stable through the hit.

This is often the reason why many youngsters and beginners of the game instantly take to the two-handed stroke. It makes the stroke easier to learn, offers more power and control on their hits, and thus motivates many to continue playing the game.

Contact with the ball can be made slightly closer to the body (not as far out in front) when

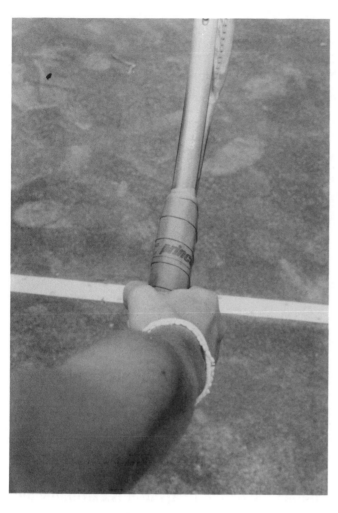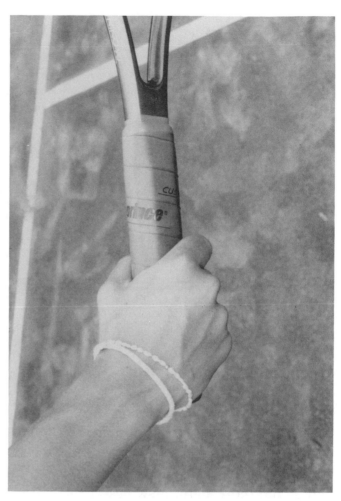

Continental backhand grip.

using two hands. This eases the backhand woes many experience. Another common backhand ailment is chopping down on the ball with a high-to-low swing. Using two hands helps stop this problem by aligning the racket back in a lower "tuck" position, giving a smooth, flowing low-to-high swing.

Even though it may appear that I'm touting a two-handed backhand over a one-handed, I'm not. The advantages are certainly clear with the two-handed backhand but there are several disadvantages with this style as well. With both hands on the handle, reach is reduced and the flexibility to play a variety of shots becomes limited. Many youngsters lacking the strength have little choice with which

backhand they should use in learning the game. As they grow older and stronger, however, both backhands should be tested to discover which feels better and is right for their style of play.

THE SERVE

The serve is the game's most important stroke. Half of all the games played in singles can be decided by this stroke, depending on how well you serve in the matches you play. The service is the one stroke in which you have complete control. You can prepare to hit the shot at your own pace without having to react to your

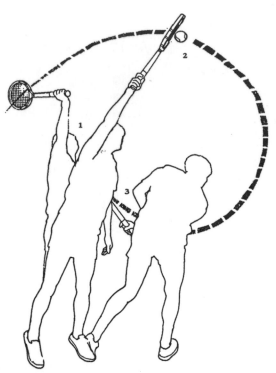

In the serve, the player is swinging up from the backswing (1) to fully extend for a proper contact overhead (2). The follow-through of the stroke allows the dominant hip and shoulder to pivot into the stroke and rest comfortably in front of the body as the racket and arm continue in a path crossing the body (3).

opponent's strike of the ball as you do for all other strokes in tennis.

Beginners of the game fear the serve as a complex stroke requiring a unison of body movements to execute properly. Although it may appear intricate and difficult, it is really one of the more natural swings at the ball in tennis. The swing is that of a relaxed overhead "throw," similar to throwing a baseball, football, or other object overhead. The non-dominant hand simply tosses the ball in the air to the precise spot that keeps the swing natural. This allows contact to occur where normally the release takes place during a throw. The difficulty at first is usually getting the two arms in sync with one another to time the hit properly. Many players have problems trying to achieve accuracy in the toss from the non-dominant hand, which is unaccustomed to such required coordinated precision.

Grip

The Continental grip is the ideal grip for the serve since it is the one that allows the most racket head movement on the hit. Beginners usually find this grip awkward at first. They often prefer to use the Eastern forehand grip while serving, as it appears easier to square the racket head up at contact with this grip. An Eastern forehand grip may make it easier to contact the ball at first, but it is extremely limited in advancing a youngster's serve. This is why the Continental is recommended as early as possible in a young player's life. The serving experience should certainly not be a devastating one to any junior player, so an Eastern might be used at first with a gradual move to a Continental.

To align the racket face properly at contact with a Continental grip, a player needs to learn to open the forearm on the swing upward. This allows you to meet the ball and then rotate your wrist outward to accelerate the racket through the ball. This can be demonstrated by facing a fence and swinging up to meet the fence overhead with a flattened racket face at contact. To do so, the hand and forehand have to open or you will contact the fence with the side of your hand and racket.

Due to the position of the arm, to drive the ball the contact of the backhand stroke must be farther in front of the body than the forehand stroke. Notice the difference in the two players' simulated contact.

This is often the reason why many beginners have trouble with the Continental grip on serves. They simply haven't learned to open the forearm to make proper contact overhead. Once this technique is discovered, the Continental grip will help them add more power to their serve by allowing the racket to move more freely and their wrist to rotate more, thus speeding the racket through the hit.

Stance

The server's stance begins behind the baseline diagonally across from the intended service box. Feet should rest comfortably shoulder width apart with the body sideways to the net. The serving arm is farthest away from the court. Hands and rackets are held together in front of the body, waist high, and towards the

court. The server's eyes should be fixed on the targeted service box across the net. The server is poised and ready to begin the point.

Motion

The arms begin in unison, both dropping down and then extending up and away from one another. The tossing arm goes towards the court and the racket-swinging arm moves towards the back fence before rising up behind the body to extend overhead and make contact with the ball.

Both arms should be relaxed and loose to help create a fluid and flowing motion for the serve. The motion should remain continuous, without any hitches or pauses through contact with the ball as well as the follow-through. This smooth motion lets the racket and arm come

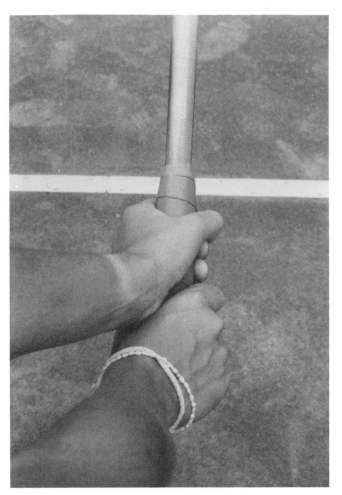
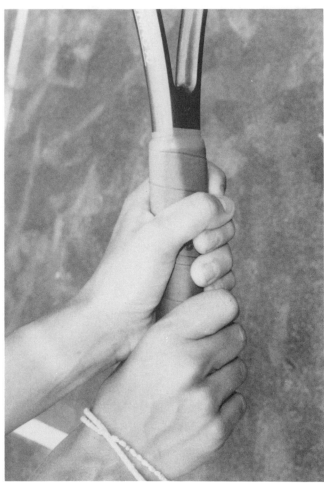

Two-handed backhand grip.

The two-handed backswing (on the right) is ideally prepared in a tuck position, ready to direct the ball with a low-to-high swing. The one-handed backswing (on the left) must loop or drop down to come under the ball to lift the shot over the net.

The server's stance.

down and cross over in front of the body after the hit has taken place.

Toss

The ball toss on the serve is crucial to keep the swing natural and smooth-flowing. When the ball is tossed to undesirable locations overhead, awkward and uncoordinated movements must be made by the serving arm and racket in an attempt to make contact with the ball. The results are often disastrous. To master a consistent toss may take time, but it will be well worth it in the long run. Without it, your serve will lack the fluidity and natural swing at the ball necessary to serve consistently well.

The toss should be placed approximately as high as your outstretched racket can reach overhead, a comfortable distance in front of the body, and slightly to the dominant side of the server (i.e., to the right of a right-handed player).

To hold the ball properly on the toss, cradle it with your fingers and release it with a "push" as the arm fully extends up overhead. Avoid "flicking" it up at a lower point using the wrist or elbow as a lever. This causes the ball to lose its accuracy and certainly will lead to inconsistent toss placements.

The Stroke

To hit the ball over the net, you must learn to *hit up* on your serve. This is probably the single most misunderstood aspect of the stroke. So many players net their serves and are perplexed

The toss is an important element of the serve. The tossing arm of the player acts like a lever to push (or extend) up for controlled placements overhead.

as to what happened! Simply hitting down on the ball with a downward angle of the racket face at contact causes the ball to go into the net.

A player does have two chances to get the ball into play with the serve — the *first serve* and the *second serve*. In the early stages, both should be played with identical motions, with the second serve cautiously directed into the service box. This doesn't mean you should "boom" your first serve and "float" your second. Just snap your racket with less force on the second serve to place the ball consistently into the target area.

Many beginners always keep a firm wrist throughout the serve. They could in all likelihood hit a much harder ball if they would relax their arms and wrists. The racket must do

more of the work instead of forcing the arm to do it all. As the server reaches up with a fully extended arm at contact, the racket continues traveling through the ball as the wrist rotates and the arm slows down for optimum power and control on the serve.

Learn to take your time on your serve. Don't be so anxious to rush into the stroke. This is one of the major differences between the juniors and the professionals. The pros never rush! Watch them. They'll bounce the ball several times, take a deep breath and feel completely ready and comfortable in their service stance before *every serve*.

Practice to find your own rhythm for effective services. Slight variations in ball tosses and swings affect the motion and the place-

The receiver's stance or ready position when preparing to receive serve.

The volley position or ready position when playing the net.

ment of the serves. Strive to develop a stroke that feels both smooth and flowing but especially one that is natural for you.

THE RETURN-OF-SERVE

If the serve is the most important stroke in tennis, what is the second most important? You guessed it . . . the return-of-serve. While half of all games in tennis can be decided by the serve, the same can also be said of the *return-of-serve.*

The return-of-serve is played with either a forehand or a backhand. The stroke may have to be modified slightly if the serve is coming faster. This is achieved by shortening the swing

for a more compact hit at the ball. Quick feet and intense reactions off an opponent's serve may also be necessary for comfortable (early) contacts and controlled returns.

The ready position for the return-of-serve (as discussed earlier in this chapter) should be assumed in a location bisecting the service box in a straight line between you and the server. This will offer the best possible angle for high percentage return-of-serves. The main objective for the receiver is just that: to get a high percentage of returns into play. The more advanced the player, the more accurate and aggressive the returns can become, but consistency plays the most important factor at every level.

The grip players should wait with depends

The volley stroke is finished with only a short block swing.

A correct volley stroke has little racket movement. Notice how far in front of the body the player hits the ball.

largely on the players themselves. Continental players will obviously have only one grip, while players who switch grips from forehand to backhand will probably need to choose one grip, and be prepared to instantly change grips should the ball be directed to the other side. Some players prefer to wait with a "neutral grip" while returning serves. The only problem is that they must quickly find the correct grip for each return of serve. Beginners may experience difficulties in finding enough time to do all the necessary steps successful returns require: finding the right grip, preparing the racket, moving the feet, executing good early contacts. There is, however, sufficient time for all this, even when serves are forcefully directed. It will just take practice.

The number one problem with players' returns is that many neglect to practice them enough. The shot is the second most important in tennis and directly affects half of all games, yet rarely is it given the time and concern it so rightfully deserves.

Learn to shorten your stroke and move towards the ball to strike it early and in front of your body. Raise your intensity to match the speed at which the ball is served to you. Quickly find your grip and the foot speed necessary to prepare yourself and your racket for comfortable hits. Through practice you can achieve the high percentage return-of-serves you desire.

THE VOLLEY

Playing a ball in the air before it bounces is considered a volley stroke no matter where the stroke occurs on court. The majority of all volleys, however, will be played in the forecourt near the net. This is when aggressive players race towards the net and play opponents' shots back with a volley, often returning them quicker than opponents are prepared for.

Grip

The grip you should use for volleying will largely depend on your playing level. Beginners often find the Eastern forehand and backhand grip preferable since the wrist is firmer, offering more stability on hits. As your level of play increases, it will become more obvious how difficult it is to change grips at the net when rapid exchanges occur. This is why it is recommended to use the Continental grip while volleying at the net. It offers the most flexibility in your feel for the ball at the net, plus it won't require grip changes for playing balls off either side or overhead. Even at the beginning level, if you have enough strength to adjust and lock your wrist when volleying, the Continental grip should be the grip to use.

Stroke

Many players don't like to volley because they have a fear of the net position. The ball comes faster to them there (since they're closer to opponents) and they don't feel quick enough to handle the shots played to them. It's important to learn to like to volley at an early age since there will be times in tennis when either you will find yourself at the net or you will need to get up there in order to win the point. The volley is really one of the easiest strokes in tennis to play; it just requires correct technique to be executed properly.

The first thing to learn about volleying is that the racket should move as little as possible before, during, and after the hit. For the backswing, the shoulders merely pivot, cocking the racket only slightly back into the correct position, ready for early contacts in front of the body. Remember from earlier discussions that the backswing is only for preparation and power. When volleying, quick preparation is essential, and little power is needed since players are positioned so close to the net.

The volley stroke is played more with a "punch" or "block" swing, which places the racket face out to meet the ball in front of the body. The racket face angle dictates the direction of the shot, so minimal swing is necessary to place the ball accurately. This shortened, uncomplicated motion helps to lessen the higher margin for error in volley hits. Just like in baseball, when the catcher holds the glove still he has a better chance of catching the ball than if he swings his glove while attempting to catch it.

Essentials

On the volley, the racket head should always remain higher than the wrist. This upright, locked wrist position will help to add valuable racket stability and control. When shots are played low at your feet, the racket itself shouldn't be lowered to contact the ball; *the entire body lowers* to make the shot. This helps to keep the firm wrist and control of the ball, even on difficult low volleys.

The ready position for the volley is essentially the same as for groundstrokes, except the heightened intensity level at the net calls for a keener sense of readiness. Players should come off their heels and stand more on the balls of their feet, flex their knees slightly, and shift their weight more to the front of the body. The arms should extend farther away from the body to prepare for quick, compact swings at the ball.

The feet are ready to move diagonally at the net by crossing over after the shoulders have made their pivot to prepare the racket. And following each volley hit, quick movement should occur that will recoil the player back into position, ready to play the next ball directed their way. An important point to remember is *go to the ball* when volleying. Don't wait for it to come to you. Successful volleyers time their movements and extend their racket out to meet the ball in front before it has the chance to reach them by simply waiting for it.

SUMMARY

Establishing good habits in tennis begins with the ready position. The difference in the levels of players is often what takes place *before* and *after* the shots they've played, not necessarily the shots of the players themselves. The most essential element in the forehand and backhand stroke is the contact, since it is here that control of the ball takes place. Early contact with the ball is vital for backhand hits, but successful players learn to contact the ball early, in front of the body on either side. A "seven-ball" follow-through helps to keep the racket face at the proper angle throughout the hit. This directs the ball with consistent control. The loop backswing is preferred to improve rhythm and power when timing allows; however, both the loop and the straight-back are important to learn and to execute. The two-handed backhand (and in some instances, the two-handed forehand) may be the easiest way to learn the stroke correctly.

The serve is the game's most important stroke. Although it may appear difficult, the serve is really played quite naturally. When both arms work together properly, a correctly tossed ball allows for a natural motion on the hit as if the server were throwing the racket. The game's second most important shot is the return-of-serve. The more advanced the level of play, the more aggressive and accurate the returns can become, but consistency will always be the most important factor.

The racket should move as little as possible before, during, and after volley hits. It's really easy to volley once you've learned the correct, compact technique required.

Chapter 3

DEVELOPING THE FUNDAMENTALS

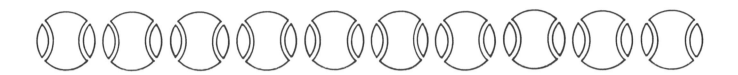

BALL AND COURT SENSE

For younger players, three to eight years of age, and for older, beginning-level juniors, the initial exposure to the fundamentals of the game should center more around ball skills and active fun than actual play. This is when ball sense and feel for the ball are being developed, along with eye-hand coordination. In the early stages, becoming comfortable with a racket in hand on the court is the most important thing, along with simply having FUN on the court!

Here are some ball skills you can practice alone:

❑ Balance the ball on the racket face.

❑ Bounce the ball up on the racket face.

❑ Bounce the ball down to the court from the racket face.

❑ Bounce the ball up on the racket face, then down to the ground, alternating between the two.

❑ Bounce the ball up on alternating faces of the racket.

You can first do these all while standing still. When you feel confident with that, practice them while walking around the tennis court.

There are more ball skills you can practice with another person:

❑ Easy Rally. Gently bounce or hit the ball with one another on court at short range and without a net.

❑ Toss-Hit-Catch. One person (without racket) tosses the ball to the other, who hits the ball back to the tosser with either a forehand or backhand.

❑ Easy Volley. Gently tap ball back and forth in the air without a bounce and without a net.

❑ Toss-Volley-Catch. One person (without a racket) tosses the ball to the other, who hits the ball back to the tosser with either a forehand or backhand volley.

All ball skill drills should be practiced using the correct forehand, backhand, or volley grips. Each drill can also be made into a game to make them it fun or challenging. For example, how many "ups" can you do while walking around the court one time? How many rallies can we do together before one misses? Once players exhibit good feel for the ball and coordination in controlling hits, their success in playing the game will certainly be that much more enhanced, and they will enjoy tennis all the more for it.

Tennis baseball and other such games can help keep the fun in learning the fun-damentals of tennis.

THE IMPORTANCE OF GOOD FOOTWORK

Famed junior tennis coach, Nick Bolletieri, says he looks for three things in determining a youngster's potential talent in the game: the desire to win, a good attitude, and most important, *footwork*.

Your feet line you up for proper contact with the ball. It's just that simple. The pros make the game look so easy because their footwork is so very good. They line up correctly for each shot over and over again without having to make uncoordinated body moves and stabs at the ball while trying to reach it like many lower level players do. They understand the importance of good footwork and let their feet do the work in bringing out successful play in themselves. They are able to "groove their strokes," hitting similar shots over and over again, by lining up in the ideal position to play each shot.

Top tennis professionals Michael Chang and Steffi Graf have built their reputations on quick feet. They constantly bounce while on court, taking many tiny steps to align themselves properly — even for balls that are directed straight to them!

Junior players should take note from these two great champions. When playing, learn to bounce on the balls of your feet to be ready to propel your body in the direction of the hit. The closer you are to the ball, the shorter and quicker your steps should become to allow exact body position for comfortable hits. Even balls that are directed right to you should require several tiny steps. On balls farther away, lengthen your first strides but then shorten your steps as you prepare closer to the hit. After you've made contact with the ball, quicken your steps once again to get back in the ready position to continue play of the point.

Players wishing to advance their game should make a commitment to reach all balls on court. Your capacity to reach just one extra ball and send it back across the net could raise your game another notch. This may require you to get into shape because when you commit to reach all balls on court, you must be prepared to keep this up for an entire match.

The first thing that you can usually look for when stroking problems develop is slow-moving feet. This is why so many professionals of the game train so hard to keep their tennis

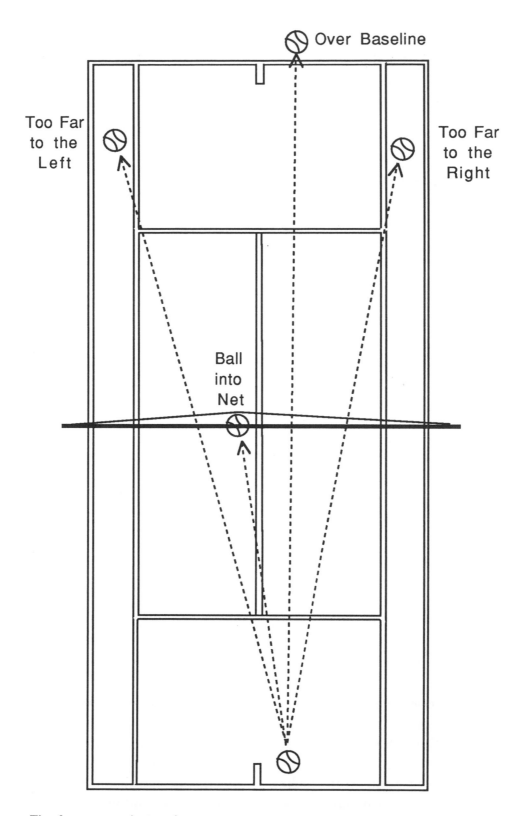

The four errors in tennis.

play at the highest level. They too have made the commitment to reach all balls on court and fully intend to uphold this commitment, no matter how many miles they have to run during the match they play.

GAINING CONTROL OF THE BALL

Although all of the great players in tennis history have learned the importance of quick feet, they have also learned that once they reach the ball it is equally important to use a correct swing to direct the ball with control. A *quick feet, slow racket* rule of thumb should be used to help develop smoother flowing strokes once your strides line you up correctly for the shot.

Players with slow or sluggish feet will, in all probability, always struggle with control of the ball in tennis. They will continue to "whip" or "flick" at the ball in an attempt to return it since their feet haven't properly set them up for a comfortable hit. If they would only hasten their footwork, they would soon discover that it would be much easier to control the ball by taking a slower swing at it.

Shots in tennis are often missed when they are rushed or hurried. I see this as the number one problem in junior tennis. Young players are often so impatient — ready to risk it all and end the point in a hurry. They swing wildly at the ball and wonder why their rate of success remains so low. They haven't learned to use a *controlled swing to hit a controlled ball.*

To have a swing that is more effective, let it become more efficient. Slow your swing down and concentrate on a long contact. Let the force of your swing send your racket through the ball. A flowing, rhythmic stroke can drive the ball with a lot less effort and yet produce better results in the process.

Overhitting with wasted power and energy is senseless. Once your feet have quickly pre-pared you for the hit, slow down your swing to gain better control. Don't try so hard when stroking the ball. Relax . . . and let your racket flow smoothly through the ball. You can gain better control by learning to match the effort of your swing to the task of the shot.

ERRORS WIN THE POINTS

Most points in a tennis match are over after only three to four hits. At every level, the majority of points won are off *errors*, not winners. Even at the professional level, approximately 70% of all points are won due to errors. It follows that as the level of expertise of the players decreases, the percentage of points won from errors will increase accordingly.

The best way to understand errors is to learn the four mistakes in tennis. They are: hitting the ball *into the net*; hitting the ball *over the baseline;* hitting the ball *too far to the right;* or hitting the ball *too far to the left.* Once you've made contact with the ball, these are the only four errors you can make playing the game. The object is then to avoid making one of these four mistakes by learning to keep the ball in play. Even though it is a very basic premise, it is one that is easily forgotten.

The net is where the majority of errors are made in tennis. The best tactic to use to avoid making this error is simply to aim *two nets high* when making shots. By swinging low-to-high, the ball will clear the net with a greater safety margin, allowing fewer errors to be made into the net. This "lifting" of the ball on your strokes will help to insure success over the net — often the number one obstacle in tennis.

Other common errors are made when players aim too close to the side or baseline on their hits. A tip to remember is: "Aim a yard from the line and you'll be fine!" By allowing a comfortable margin for error on all of your hits, you will help to avoid making unnecessary errors that occur when your aim is too close to the net or the lines.

In tennis, errors can either be *forced* or *unforced*. A forced mistake occurs when an opponent hits a shot that is too difficult to handle. An unforced error is more of a routine shot that is missed because it is played carelessly. You should attempt to avoid all errors. Reducing the number of unforced errors is the best place to begin.

The typical tennis match is made up of two players trying to give each other the game by making a series of errors, until finally someone succeeds in giving the match away. The winner feels like he has won the match because he was the better player, while the loser feels he lost because he has beaten himself. Although each may be right in his assessment, probably the loser just gave the match away first! Remember, most matches are *lost*, not won. The player with the fewest errors in the end is the usual victor.

CONSISTENCY AND ACCURACY SEPARATE THE LEVELS IN TENNIS

The consistently winning pros, the ones who make it into the finals week after week, understand percentage tennis play. It is a common misconception that the pros hit very low to the net and aim for the lines on most strokes. But in fact, this is not true. They will place the ball close to the net and the lines only if the match situation calls for these lower percentage shots. Normally their placements are 3 to 6 feet above the height of the net and several feet away from the sidelines and baseline. They play aggressively only when necessary; however, they don't gamble unreasonably. By playing percentage tennis, they reduce the number of errors they make in the matches they play and by doing so, win more on a regular basis.

Your ultimate tactic in tennis should therefore be consistency, no matter at what level you play the game. Consistent tennis players are the toughest ones to beat because they are the ones who won't beat themselves! The big hitters, risk-takers, and flashy shot artists are rarely the consistently winning players in the game. They might score on an unbelievable shot here and there, but they will usually beat themselves with all the errors they make in the process.

Players who use smooth, reliable strokes and keep the ball comfortably away from the net and lines won't likely be the ones to make the first error in the points they play. They understand that successful tennis begins with letting opponents make the first error, and they won't attempt to beat them to it!

The next time you're practicing, try hitting five strokes before you attempt to win the point. This will help you learn to keep the ball in play longer. It will also help you get better rhythm and control from your strokes in the longer rallies created. You will discover that your consistent control of the ball will make you into the consistently winning player you desire to be. Keep in mind that crosscourt shots are better at reducing errors. The net is 6 inches lower in the center of the court and there are approximately 6½ more feet of court to hit into on the crosscourt angle, as compared to the down-the-line shots (78 feet versus 84½ feet).

Every shot in tennis should be hit with a purpose in mind. A *target* must be conceived in the player's mind before a hit is made to be able to accurately place the ball there. Balls aren't directed aimlessly about the court in hopes of good fortune. They are predetermined, or predirected, by the players involved.

Tennis is said to be a game of inches, and

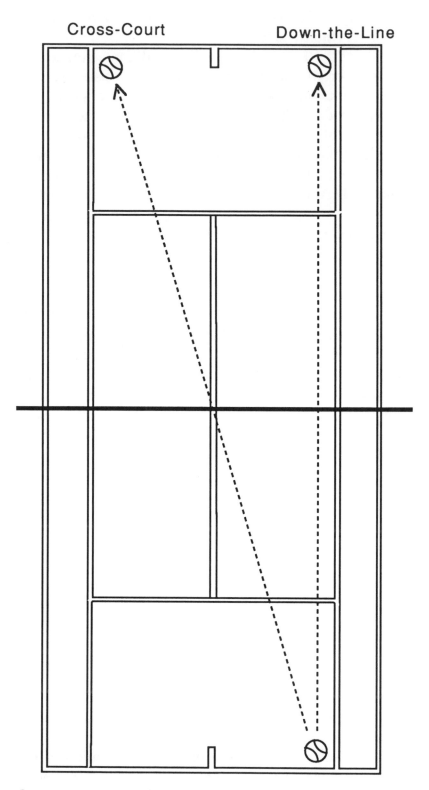

Cross-court versus down-the-line.

Practicing in the alley will help players develop better control by learning to hit the ball in a straight line.

players often use every inch of the court with their shots. Although a comfortable margin is suggested for consistent hits, to place the ball accurately closer to the net or lines (when necessary) is what advanced control of the ball is all about.

To place the ball accurately with better control, learn to hit the ball in a straight line. From your stance and shoulder position to your racket backswing, prepare your swing to follow to your intended target in a straight line. Your follow-through should point the ball's path with a long and extended contact that aids the control and accuracy of your hit. When going crosscourt, simply line the body and racket up to direct the ball in a straight line, only this time diagonally across the court. Once you are able to control the ball in a straight line, you will be able to place it as accurately as necessary to targets all over the court.

LEARNING TO GIVE 100%

Even though correct strokes are so important in the development of a sound tennis game, nothing will take you further in this sport than sheer *desire and determination*. It is true that great strokes can mold a person into a player, but unless 100% effort is applied on court, the player will never be much of a formidable opponent.

I've always believed that the most determined player in tennis is the usual victor. Since this statement says nothing of the player's strokes or ability level, it actually won't always hold true. But if you had two players of equal skills and ability levels competing, with one determined to win and giving 100% total effort, while the other is competing with minimal desire, the outcome of the match would be completely one-sided. This is how important maximum effort is in achieving the best play in yourself. It can sway a match in your favor simply by focusing your energy and desire into giving 100% on court.

The top competitors in tennis today have the right attitude and work ethic concerning their tennis play. They realize that they will get back only what they put forth, so they are prepared to work hard and give it their all each time they play the game. They opt to give no less than 100% effort every time they step onto the court. They understand that they could probably give less on occasion but they rarely will succumb to this since they have no intention of lowering the goals they've set for themselves. Lower-level players don't usually share the same work ethic as those who have succeeded to the top. They will often continue to search for "the secret to successful play" without realizing that it has been within them all the while in the form of determination and focused 100% effort.

Practicing less than 100% will usually cause you to play that way during matches. This is why most tennis problems occur on the *practice court*. In a match, balls are not allowed to bounce twice, so when rallying in practice, don't let it happen either! Give it your all to reach the ball before it bounces twice — that means whether the ball lands either in or out of bounds on the practice court. Develop an enthusiasm for giving 100% during practice time and you will discover that this winning mentality will become a natural, instinctive part of you every time you play the game. You'll become the determined player who will also be the usual victor!

BUILDING YOUR GAME ON A SOLID FOUNDATION

Everyone experiences "off days" in tennis when nothing seems to go right, the feeling just isn't there, or the feet feel like lead! Take a tip from the pros and learn to do as they do — *go back to the basics* when your game goes awry.

If your tennis game is built on a solid foundation — you have a good understanding for the game and are able to execute properly good control of the ball — you can never really be in trouble with your game. Your play may vary on certain days, but remembering to go back to the basic "contact with the ball" when errors occur will help you to gain control over your strokes and return to your winning form.

To believe in your basics you must have strokes you can count on. This is why a limited number of strokes that you can rely on completely is better than possessing a huge arsenal of strokes. Players with a full range of shots may be fully confident in none of them, while players with fewer strokes — but ones that are accurate and consistent — have developed a more solid foundation to build a winning game from.

Reliable strokes are developed through repetition and consistency. This is why practice is so vitally important in stroke development. Unfortunately there are no short-cuts to stroke greatness. This is why the old adage, "Practice, practice, practice" still rings true today. For consistent stroke placements, the safety margin must also be figured in to allow for a comfortable height above the net and placements well within the boundary lines on the court.

The very base of your game should be built on an understanding of how and why errors occur. If you learn to analyze errors correctly, when you make them you will never be at a loss for how to correct them. Unintelligent tennis players have yet to learn this secret of using their minds on the court. They will continue to struggle with inconsistent play because of it.

Complete control of the ball is the most sound foundation to build a winning game from. Contact with the ball and a lengthened contact during the stroke follow-through dictate where the shot will be directed off of the face of the racket. Proper footwork sets up your body for comfortable hits, while a controlled swing hits a controlled ball. Go back to this basic fundamental if you find your strokes "off" on a given day. If you've built your game on a solid foundation, you'll never be at a loss for how to gain your control back.

SUMMARY

For beginning-level players, ball skills and active fun are more important than actual play. Being comfortable on the court and having fun in the process is the best way to begin learning the fundamentals of tennis.

Your feet can make all the difference in your game. The pros make the game look so easy because they move their feet so well and line up correctly for every shot. Learn to do as they do. Bounce on the balls of your feet — like a boxer or jump-roper — to move more quickly and stroke more comfortably. Even though your feet will be quick, remember that once you reach the ball, use a slow swing to direct the ball with control.

The majority of all points in tennis are won off errors, not winners. Understand that there are only four mistakes in tennis, and the object is to avoid making them. Your ultimate tactic in tennis should always be consistency. Successful tennis begins with letting opponents make the first error.

Although developing good strokes is important, nothing can take you further in the game of tennis than learning to give 100% effort. Every time you step onto the court be prepared to give nothing less. If you ever find yourself in trouble, go back to the basics of sound control of the ball. You'll experience far fewer off-days in tennis if your game has been built on a solid foundation of understanding control of the ball.

Chapter 4

ADVANCED SHOT MAKING

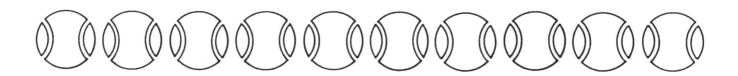

SPINS, POWER, AND DEPTH

Once you have developed reliable forehand and backhand strokes that exhibit good control of the ball, you will then be ready to advance your strokes to a higher quality of ball control through *spins*, *depth*, and *power*.

Spin

Spin of the ball occurs at contact as the strings of the racket "brush" the backside of the ball, either upward for topspin, downward for underspin, or across the ball for sidespin. The amount of spin will vary according to the length of contact and force of the swing. A shorter length of contact — a quick brush — generates more spin as the racket "edges" the ball, causing it to rotate in the direction of the racket path. Longer contacts drive the racket through the ball more solidly and will give less spin on the ball but can offer players better controlled hits. Exact timing is necessary to control shots hit with spin. The professionals who play the game for a living understand this and that is one of the major reasons they practice daily to keep their timing and game sharp.

Topspin has changed the game of tennis as we know it today. It has had such a profound effect on the styles and strategies of players that to see a leading player scoring success without the use of topspin would be most unusual. Topspin's popularity has grown primarily because tennis has become such a power game. A topspinning ball rotates forward and downward, which helps to bring the ball into the court once it has cleared the net. Balls can be struck much harder when topspin is applied and still remain within the boundary lines. Flat hit balls (without spin) must rely on gravity to keep the ball in play.

Topspin. The racket travels from beneath the ball and finishes high, brushing up the back of the ball. This lifting motion allows the ball to clear the net with a good margin but still land within the boundary lines as the topspin of the ball pulls it down onto the court.

Topspin Drive. The racket travels through the ball in a straighter drive and then gradually lifts up to give topspin during the follow-through, which is farther in front. The longer contact helps to add control to the hit and more power to the stroke, as the force of the swing travels more into the ball.

Topspin Roll. The racket rolls over the ball to create topspin on the hit. This stroke is often the result of higher-played balls or players being closer to the net and in a position to hit down on the ball. Otherwise, this is not the ideal topspin stroke to play.

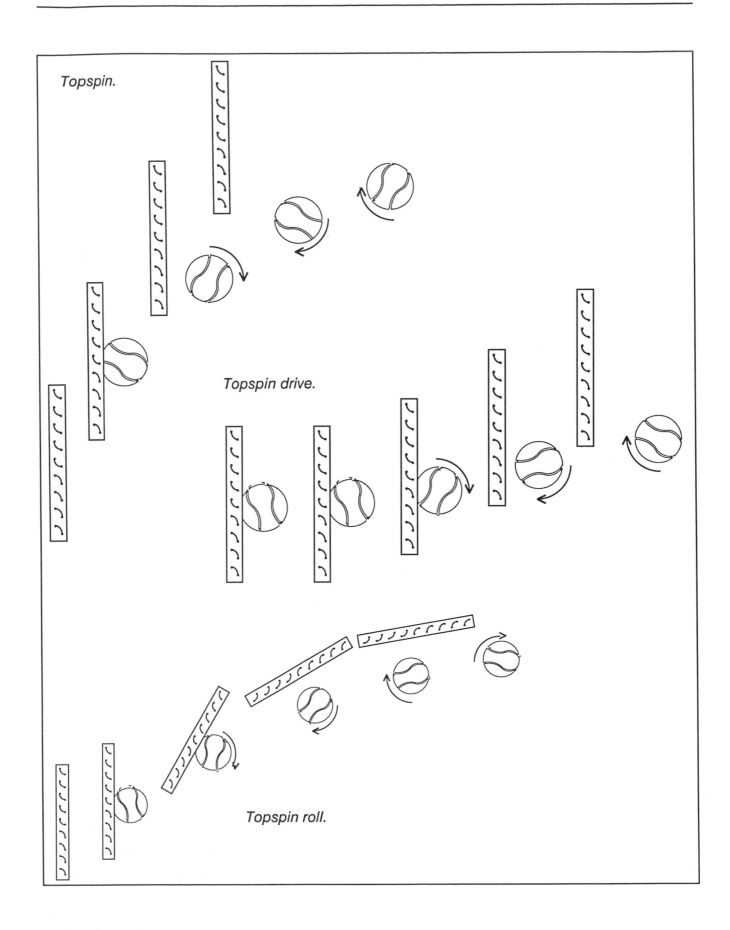

Topspin.

Topspin drive.

Topspin roll.

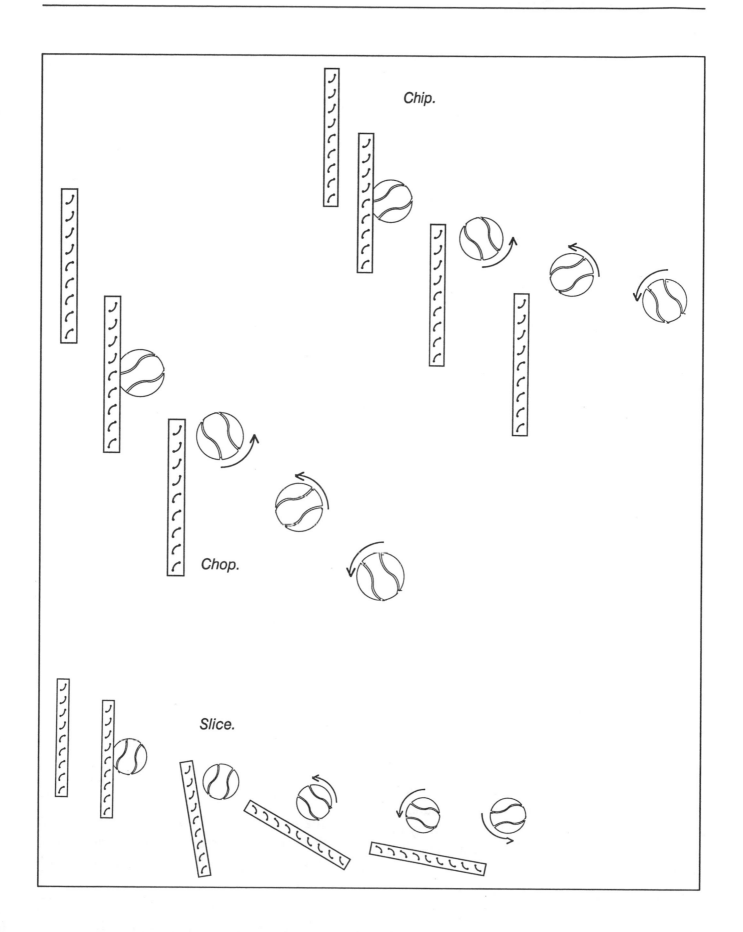

An underspinning ball, on the other hand, often tends to stay in flight longer. It spins in the opposite rotation from a topspinning ball since the ball is struck with a downward moving racket. It is this backspin of the ball that can create a drag in airflow underneath, often times keeping it afloat a little longer than normal.

Chip. The racket moves downward in a shortened stroke. The angle of the swing and the compact "follow-through" direct the ball low over the net and usually short in the court.

Chop. The racket travels down the back of the ball in an extreme high-to-low swing. Even though a lot of spin can be created using a chop, it is not a recommended stroke since exact timing is required or the ball will tend either to "pop" up or end in the bottom of the net.

Slice. The racket travels from a slightly high to a low swing, but in a long and smooth follow-through that directs the ball with control. The racket face opens upon impact just slightly to allow the downward brush of the ball for underspin.

Inside-Out or Reverse Court. The racket brushes across the ball sideways as it comes off the face of the racket. A ball directed inside-out is usually played to bounce away from an opponent. It is a stroke that is normally used by players who tend to run around a particular stroke and find themselves on the other half of the court hitting the ball.

Balls hit with spin tend to bounce differently when they strike the court. Topspinning ones will "kick up" upon hitting the court surface, while underspinning balls slide lower, not bouncing nearly as high as a regular bouncing ball would. Side-spinning balls may bounce as high as usual but will generally move away in a "curved path" as opposed to remaining in a straight line.

Power

Power has become the name of the game in tennis! Everyone wants it. But power without control is useless, so it's really *controlled power* that you're after to advance your shot-making skills.

Contrary to popular belief, swinging harder at the ball will not necessarily hit the ball with more speed. Power lies in the technique and timing used to get your racket into the proper position to make contact with the ball. Usually a smooth, graceful, but well-timed hit will generate more ball speed than a wild, free-swinging one. The reason lies in solid contact with good racket control. Balls can be hit at a higher speed by simply allowing more force from the swing to be directed into sending the ball over the net. This efficiency can actually be quite effective at generating power to the ball on hits. It won't necessarily require more speed from your swing either.

Wristy players whip a lot of power into their shots, but rarely with sufficient control. This is the reason a firm wrist is very important for controlling powerful groundstrokes and volleys.

To achieve more power off the ground, be sure that your backswing has been taken far enough back to sufficiently supply the force needed. A shortened backswing will generally lack the forward momentum needed for powerful shot making unless you have timed your hit extremely well and used your opponent's pace.

A body that is well-positioned and well-balanced is best prepared to hit a powerful shot. When properly aligned behind the ball, the body is best-positioned to give stability to the shot and generate force by moving forward into the hit. The shoulders and hips are able to rotate better and pivot into the shot, in the process accelerating the racket through the ball for added power.

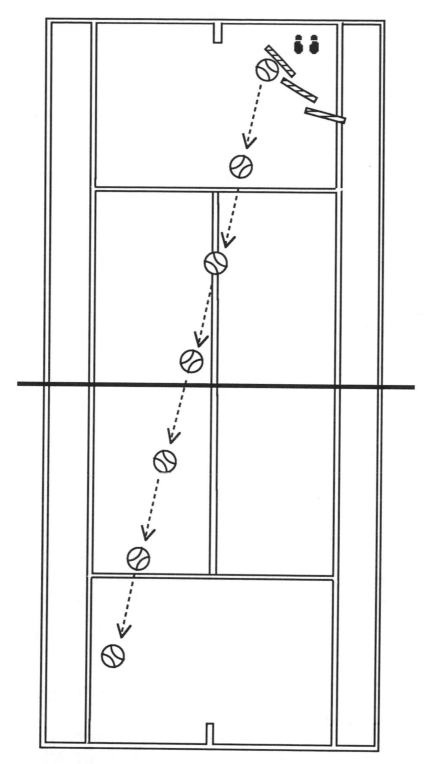

Reverse court.

Depth

The advanced form of placement in tennis is depth. A ball that is hit deep in the court (closer to the baseline) is a much more difficult shot to handle. On the other hand, balls that land short in the court, closer to the net or midcourt, are handled with relative ease. This is why higher level players use shot placements to advance their games. They place the ball within several feet of the baseline and force opponents to make weak or poor returns from there.

To find the right depth, adjust the net clearance path of your shots. Allow a good margin for error by not taking aim directly at the baseline but instead a yard inside. Work to add spins, power, and depth to your hits to increase the quality of control you have over the ball.

LEARNING TO MAKE STROKE ADJUSTMENTS

The term "grooved strokes" is used when players are into a rhythm, stroking the ball similarly over and over again until they are swinging at the ball as if they are in automatic. This ideal state comes about when one of two things is taking place (or both): 1) opponents are hitting the same type of shot (speed, direction, placement), or 2) players have good footwork, anticipation, and preparation.

Aspiring young players who desire to advance their strokes to automatic should learn to concentrate their efforts on the latter. In other words, develop footwork, anticipation, and preparation. Nothing will help to develop smooth and flowing strokes more than these three things.

There are, however, certain times when stroking adjustments will need to be made for different shots you are about to play, as well as for different shots your opponent has played to you. This will require flexibility on your part to be able to adapt your strokes as necessary.

As a rule of thumb on your own strokes, a full-backswing is required at the baseline, a half-backswing at the midcourt, and no backswing at the net. This backswing adjustment will help to best prepare your racket for proper contacts and will also help to apply the correct amount of power needed for the strokes from these different court locations. Of course, if more power is desired, your backswing can be lengthened, and if less is required for the shot, you can shorten it accordingly.

Opponents' shots can also require adjustments to be made to your strokes. A high bouncing ball will require a backswing that must be raised for a higher contact. A lower ball needs the racket to go lower on the backswing to allow it to come from under the ball so that it clears the net. Tennis pros around the world teach "bend your knees" to return these lower shots effectively but remember, your racket must also do the lowering, not just your knees!

Different speeds and depths of your opponents' hits can also affect the way you strike the ball. Harder hit balls will force you to shorten or compact your swing, as will deeper shots, which decrease the time you have to prepare for good, early contact with the ball.

THE APPROACH SHOT

Aggressive players who love to play the game from the net position will certainly hit their share of approach shots in the matches they play. The approach shot is one of the most important shots for them. It is the final stroke that they will play from the mid- or back-court as they move forward, advancing towards the net.

As a rule of thumb, a full backswing is used at the baseline;

. . . a half backswing at the midcourt area;

. . . and no backswing at the net.

To quickly advance to the net, players move through the approach shot. Notice the racket control used as the player in the photo takes careful aim to place the ball without rushing through the shot.

The approach shot is an often misunderstood stroke in tennis. Even though it is played like a groundstroke, with either a forehand or backhand swing, the big difference is that players *move* while striking the approach shot and are *still* when playing a groundstroke. They move through the shot to quicken their approach to the net. By lowering the lead shoulder and leaning the body into the shot, players not only play the ball early out in front, but also discover that the body will move easily into the shot with the forward momentum bringing them to the net faster.

Patience and *placement* are the two keys to remember in developing your approach shot. Be patient and learn not to attempt an approach shot on all balls on your side of the court. Wait for a ball that lands short, closer to the net, so that it will be easier for you to move forward into the shot and reach the net position on your next exchange. Balls that are played deeper to you or that pull you wide out of position should be safely and patiently returned with a groundstroke, not hit with an aggressive approach shot.

To better understand which balls can be played as approach shots and which ones shouldn't, take a look at the approach shot "stop light" in the diagram. Balls that land deeper in the court and closer to the baseline — in the *red* area — should be patiently returned with a groundstroke. The *yellow* area represents "caution." If a player feels aggressive, he can still approach the net off of balls from here but he needs to take care. Unsure players should safely return the ball with a groundstroke and be patient for a *green* light ball. Balls that land in the green light area represent opportunities that signal an automatic approach shot. This is the time to "go," and players should be prepared to approach the net when green area balls strike.

Placement is the second important aspect of successful approach shots. When balls are directed deep, to the weaker stroke of opponents, or simply up the middle, it often makes for an easy volley. Approach shots are set-up shots. They are like the assist shot in other sports, which set up the winning point to be scored on the next shot. The placement of your approach shot will either *dictate* your control of the point or your loss of *control* over it. This is how important your approach shot placements are.

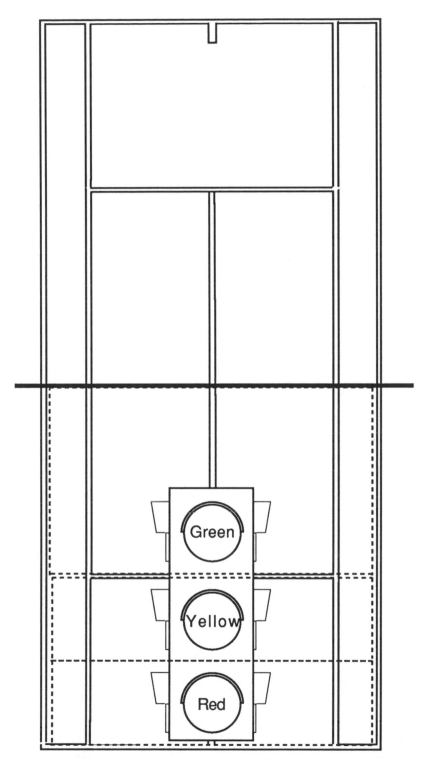

Approach shot traffic light.

Approach shot problems begin with errors. I always tell my students that approach shots are "10 for 10 shots." That is, they should be high percentage shots that you feel comfortable in making. Remember that your opponent has made a tactical error by hitting you a short ball, and you should take advantage of this opportunity, not return the favor by missing the approach shot!

Running through the shot and getting the ball off the racket too quickly are two common mistakes players make with the approach shot. Earlier I said that you should "move through the shot"; however, running through it will certainly bring its share of problems. It is important to have good balance and body control when moving slowly through the shot and to remain in control of the ball. When players hastily snap the ball off their rackets, their control over the shot decreases. Smooth swings that slide through the ball, guiding it towards a target, are what successful approach shots are all about. Consistency in the placements, along with patient and well-timed approaches, helps players to gain control over the points they play at the net.

THE HALF VOLLEY

For many, the half volley is considered one of the most difficult shots in tennis. When attempting to stroke a ball off the top of your shoes, do you choose a volley, a ground-stroke, or a stroke that lies between the two — a half volley? Do you move forward and play the ball in the air, back up and let it take a good bounce, or keep your balance and let the ball take a mini-bounce before returning it over the net? This is where most players' troubles begin ...*indecision* with which shot they should play.

The half volley is the choice shot to play for more advanced-level players. They realize the arduous task in "digging out" extremely low volleys to clear the net and still retain control of the point. They have also learned not to back up for a shot unless it is one that is over their heads. By executing a half volley, they are able to remain completely in position and still play a rather awkward ball with a controlled hit.

The first rule to remember when learning to hit half volleys effectively is that the shot should be played *defensively*. Power and winning placements should be saved for balls that are played between waist and shoulder height. Balls that are stroked from a low height, close to the ground, must have more "care" used. If not, they are more likely to end up in the net, and if too much power is applied, they can sail over the baseline with relative ease.

To prepare your body properly for a half volley hit, think that you are hitting a forehand or backhand, only lower and shorter. Because a half volley is played closer to the ground, it is vitally important that the body be lowered with a deep knee bend. This puts the racket low enough to still come from under the ball with a lifting swing so that it can clear the net. The most common error happens when players either bend at the waist and play the shot off-balance, or worse, simply drop the racket head down to scoop the ball up. The result is a "pop up" shot, which either opponents can easily hit for a winner or has uncontrolled placement.

Even though the stroke is played like the forehand or backhand hit (including the grip), the major difference is the length of the swing. A more "compact swing" is necessary to control the power of the stroke and to time the hit early in front of the body. The backswing should be shortened considerably, but the follow-through is lengthened to lift and guide the ball to deep targets or shortened to "bunt" the ball when shallower placements are attempted.

Timing seems to be what eludes most beginners in learning the stroke. They aren't ac-

The player on the left is out of balance by bending at the waist to handle the difficult half volley shot, while the player on the right is also incorrectly playing the ball at her feet by dropping the racket head down.

customed to striking the ball so quickly after it has bounced. The best way I have found for teaching the timing technique is to have my students say "babump" when learning to half volley. Say the first part of the word, "ba," when the ball hits the court and the "bump" with the immediate stroke that follows. To improve your hits, say "babump" over and over again until you understand the timing that is required. Balls that are struck immediately following the bounce should be played with a "babump" timed hit, while those taken shortly after the bounce might be played with a more "ba . . . bump."

The half volley is played with a firm wrist. This is to keep the racket in control on the swing so that the ball will not be deflected uncontrollably. The best way to do this is to keep the racket head at least parallel to the court and not allow it to drop below the wrist. The weight of the body remains in balance as the center of gravity lowers with the knee bend, but moves slowly forward through the shot as the ball is played out in front. Balls that are taken on the side of the body or are played from behind become extremely difficult to control and should be avoided if at all possible.

Half volleys are shots that are most often played from the midcourt area. This is where balls can be directed easily at players' feet. Players can, however, make half volley shots from positions all over the court. But since the shot is a difficult one and one that should be played carefully and defensively, it should only be a shot that you use when caught in the awkward position of having to play a ball directed at your feet.

THE DROP SHOT AND DROP VOLLEY

When the situation calls for a delicately placed ball, one that needs to fall short, close to the net, and out of the opponent's range, a drop shot or drop volley will be the choice shot to use.

Drop shots are not considered the highest percentage shots in the game. They actually offer a very low percentage chance of success because most players choose the wrong time to attempt the shot or lack the "feeling" necessary to score with it. The same can be said of drop volleys.

Drop shots attempted from the baseline

A correct half volley begins with a good knee bend. Players who have lowered themselves are better positioned and balanced to lift the ball accurately over the net.

area are certain to produce low percentage play. Midcourt to the net is the ideal location from which to score using drop shots and drop volleys. It is from here, in close range of the net, that the ball can be lightly hit with success to just clear the net and *die*. When such shots are tried from the baseline, opponents are given more time, which enables them to race forward and reach the short ball since it must stay in flight longer to clear the net.

Another incorrect time to drop shot is when opponents are in close range. The best time to hit a drop shot is when opponents are back behind the baseline or way out of position on either side of the sidelines. From this position they will have a difficult time in reaching a ball placed close to the net and so far away from them.

To play a drop shot, use your regular grip. Raise your backswing above the ball but shorten the stroke since little power is needed. The swing should come down the back of the ball, using a racket face that opens up to the sky at contact. This "mini scoop" motion helps to add needed backspin to the ball so it will "stop" once it reaches the other side, instead of "running" forward like it would on a regular shot without underspin.

The feeling for the shot comes from soft hands and a soft wrist. When the grip is loosened slightly at contact the racket head is able to lightly "feather through" the ball, offering a

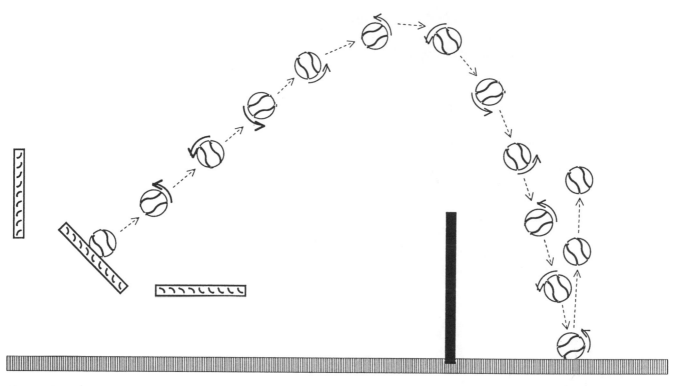

Drop shot.

delicate placement. The racket head opens at impact to bunt the ball "up" and short. On drop volleys, the racket lowers to absorb the pace and take the power out of the shot in sending it back.

Deception plays a key role in successful shot-making with drop shots. When opponents are able to read and react effectively to attempted drop shots, they are usually able to reach most of them. On the other hand, when disguise is used and the element of surprise is present, the drop shot can be a most difficult shot to reach as it is one that can be hit for a clear "winner" when well-placed.

THE LOB AND LOB VOLLEY

When properly executed, the lob is one of the most effective shots in tennis at every level. It can be a shot that is used to steal the offense away by keeping opponents at bay off the net.

The lob can even be termed an "offensive weapon" when well-placed balls clear the heads of unsuspecting net rushers and land in the open court behind them. Lobs can also be hit defensively. When players are in trouble or out of position, a lob hit high into the sky can be the ideal shot to choose. It can help to buy the necessary time to get back into position, and at the same time keep the ball in the court without making an unnecessary error.

What determines if a lob is an offensive or defensive play is the positioning of the players attempting to lob and the height of the arc in the lob they've hit. Offensive lobs are hit by players in good position and in command of the point. They are usually played off of shorter balls that easily allow players to step in behind the shot and direct it over the net rushing opponents' heads. The height of the offensive lob is a proper trajectory that, when played correctly, just clears the outstretched racket of the surprised opponent. The offensive lob

The lob can be one of the most effective shots in tennis. The player closest has just hit an offensive lob, while the far player has hit a much higher arcing defensive lob. Notice the difference in the height of the follow-through of each.

remains in the air only a short time, keeping the net player from running it down and returning it. A topspin lob offers that much more advantage as it quickly dips after it clears the net person and runs away usually untouched. This is why the lob can be an offensive shot; it is used to take control of the point or even win it outright.

When players are pulled out of the court or jammed with difficult shots, the high lob is the intelligent shot to choose. The high arc and long hang time of the defensive lob allow them the needed time to get back into position or regain control of the point. Opponents will probably be able to have a play on the lob, but the most important thing is that no errors be committed in the process. When players try to "blast" their way out of situations, unintelligent play usually results through repeated errors.

Lobs should be stroked similar to groundstrokes. Pop-ups or short floating lobs occur when players stop their swings with a bunting motion at contact. Anyone can direct a ball upward with a "punch" or "flick" but accuracy and direction require a target and a proper follow-through. The follow-through of the stroke allows the racket to continue moving through the hit and direct the ball with control in the process. When players shovel or push the ball with little or no follow-through, weak shots and ineffective lobs result.

Weaker players normally use the lob only as a defensive tactic, but even very good players often do not know how to use lobs more effectively. *Disguise* could be your ticket to more successful offensive lobs. To better disguise your

Early preparation is so important for overhead strokes. The player has prepared sideways to the net, has taken his racket into the backscratch position, and is pointing to the ball with his free arm.

lobs, strive to stroke the ball in the same manner as a groundstroke, only lift the ball a little more on the follow-through as your stroke finishes higher. Often the best surprise tactic available is lobs appearing as though they are normal forehands or backhands and then suddenly clearing the heads of unprepared opponents.

Disguised lobs also come in the form of lob volleys. A block lob, such as a lob volley, can be quite surprising when executed properly and will surely keep opponents off-balance and guessing. A lob can be made off the volley (before it bounces) by opening up the racket face and adjusting the angle and power of the hit to have the ball just clear the outstretched racket of the opponent and still land within the boundaries of the court.

THE OVERHEAD

As your tennis game advances, considerable time will usually be spent playing the net. To develop a sense of security in your ability to play the net, you need a dependable overhead stroke you feel confident with.

Many lower-level players fear the net, the lob, and their overhead stroke. They are fearful for several reasons: they practice their overhead rarely, they lack the understanding of backward mobility at the net, they aren't accustomed to judging balls overhead and have trouble with their perception, and they attempt to smash the shot and come away with inconsistent results they don't feel confident in making.

The best smashes are played overhead with a fully outstretched arm at a comfortable distance in front of the body. The stroke is played similarly to the serve; using the Continental grip, positioning the body weight behind the ball, and then swinging the arm with a natural throwing motion. Preparation for the overhead stroke begins with a shoulder turn. This is to align the body properly for its natural swing at the ball. The racket goes up and back behind the head ready to strike in a "cocked" action. The free arm becomes a guidance or "aim" arm to help sight the ball overhead. Footwork is then used by sidestepping backwards to keep the ball at a comfortable distance in front of the body for ideal contacts overhead.

Poor footwork is the cause of most overhead problems. Players who move with the ball never get into the proper position or get there only in time to make rushed, uncontrolled swings at the ball. Advanced players move faster than the ball. They anticipate where the ball should be played and quickly move to set up in this location. When quick preparation is practiced, players then have the time to set, pause, and then execute comfortably. Players with slower feet rush their strokes and make awkard arm adjustments to compensate for lack of good positioning. Advanced players with sound overheads make the adjustments with their feet and are ideally positioned on a regular basis to allow for comfortable hits.

Just as with all shots in tennis, there must first be a mental target to place the ball accurately with direction and control. Players who attempt to merely "smash" the ball — as the stroke is sometimes called — are destined to experience erratic results. Placement and control can be developed by learning the rule of *short to short* and *deep to deep*. Lobs that are hit shallow or short should be angled off short with winning overhead placements. Deeper lobs require backing up to the service line and beyond, and should be returned back deep overhead. Patience is needed for these deeper lobs. Overheads from here are not easily hit for winners, and many players err when attempt-

ing to win the point off of deeper lobs.

It is best to play most lobs *without* a bounce. Opponents will then have less time to react and prepare for the shot. However, when a lob is very high or very deep, letting the ball bounce before striking it overhead is the wise choice. Even though this gives opponents more time to prepare for and read the shot, the ball is easier to manage and control after it has taken a bounce. It also allows more time to get ideally positioned behind the ball to make accurate placements.

When power does need to be applied to the ball, it's best to let the racket do the work on the swing. As with the serve, players need to reach up and hit up to allow for net clearance, but let the racket snap the ball down to bring it in before it sails long over the baseline. The eyes should remain looking up to the contact with the ball and the chin shouldn't pull downward until after contact has taken place. Pulling the head down too soon can often send the ball into the net since the arm and racket will follow suit and come down too early as well.

UNDERSTANDING THE FULL COURT CHALLENGE

One-dimensional tennis players are destined for failure. This is because tennis offers players of the game a full court challenge. Players who become proficient at one aspect of the game can be led into a false sense of security when successes come their way. This is often the case with younger players. They develop their groundstrokes and proceed to play every match from the baseline. If their strokes are carrying them through and they are winning the matches they play, why change a winning game?!

What these players don't realize is that they are neglecting important developments in other parts of their game, such as a more effective serve or play from the net. As these players mature, it will become all the more important that they have well-rounded games they can count on. If, because of temporary successes, they choose to continue to play one-dimensionally, ultimately it will catch up with them.

This is even seen at the professional level. Rising young players experience brilliance early in their careers and then drop from the rankings faster than they rose. What happened is that the other players weren't aware of the game of this newcomer and at first were beaten by surprise. But once they learned that the games of these younger players were one-dimensional they were able to take advantage of the players' limitations. Often these players will then attempt to make a comeback by taking valuable time away from the professional tour and begin working with a coach to develop the part of the game that is missing. This can take months, sometimes even years. If only they hadn't been lured into the false sense of security with their early successes, they would have been forced to develop a more well-rounded game from the very beginning.

It is important in the early stages to develop a game that you can play from the baseline, the midcourt, and the net. There will be times when you will find yourself in all three locations and your ability to score equally well from all three will help you learn to develop an all-round game with fewer limitations from the very start.

SUMMARY

Advance your strokes with a higher quality of control through spins, power, and depth. Exact timing is necessary to control spin shots, and that is the reason the professionals of the game practice daily to keep their timing and games sharp. Remember that power without control is useless, so strive for controlled power through solid contacts and good racket control. Nothing will help you develop more smooth and flowing strokes than good footwork, anticipation, and preparation.

Patience and placement are two important reminders for successful approach shots. Use the "traffic light" theory to help you better understand which balls you should approach the net behind and which ones you shouldn't.

Balls placed at your shoe tops are difficult to master. That is the reason that half volleys should be played *defensively* and *carefully* by lowering the body and shortening your backswing. On drop shots, attempt a delicate placement by using soft hands to absorb the pace and lightly send the ball just over the net. Lobs, on the other hand, should be strokes similar to groundstrokes, with the ball lifted a little higher on the follow-through as the stroke finishes. Lobs can be hit both offensively and defensively, and it is important that you understand the difference and be able to execute each. Advanced players with sound overheads understand the importance of good footwork and let their feet make the adjustments to position themselves ideally on a regular basis. Lower-level players make awkward adjustments with their arm and racket and score inconsistently with their overhead hits because of poor footwork.

It will take maturity to develop a well-rounded game, especially if you're experiencing success with a more one-dimensional style. But the game of tennis is a full court challenge, and the winning players of tomorrow will be the ones with fewer limitations in their all-round play.

Chapter 5

WINNING STRATEGIES AND TACTICS

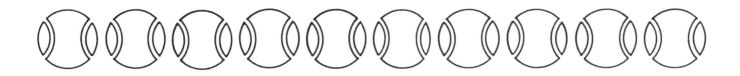

UNDERSTANDING AND PLAYING YOUR GAME

Nothing can bring you more consistent results than simply understanding your game and playing within it. Everyone has likes and dislikes, commonly known as strengths and weaknesses. Get to know yours. Be aware of your capabilities and limitations before attempting shots that you're unable to execute. This is the first step toward developing your own game style. The next important step will be to attempt to play within yourself or to play the game you are capable of. This will help you achieve consistent results on court.

Rising young players often view themselves as being able to make any and all shots in the book. Even though these players appear confident on the outside, inside their confidence and esteem levels are generally quite low. This is because they have yet to discover their own game, so they don't know how to play within it. To be able to score succcss with strategies and game plans, you must first know your game and plan strategies that suit your style of play. Don't imagine you're some player you're not. Instead, try to be the person you are, understand who that person is, and then plan and play your game as that person.

Professional tennis players have reached their level of play by realizing their capabilities and playing within them. Even though tour veterans like Steffi Graf and Ivan Lendl have been champions for many years doesn't mean they can hit any shot any time they like. They know their games and their limitations and play within them.

Errors are often made in matches when players attempt a shot they shouldn't. This regularly happens to players who are unsure of their games or style of play. If only these players understood their strengths and weaknesses and learned to play the shots they are most capable of, they would discover much more consistent success on the tennis court. They would make fewer errors, have more reliable strokes, and become more confident players in the process — all because they have learned the secret of playing and winning by using their own game.

DEVELOPING THE GAME PLANS

The worst fault that many junior tennis players have is that their strategy is simply "hitting the yellow ball." These youngsters have yet to discover the importance of the mental aspects of the game and how it can be used to benefit their play. Tennis is similar to other sports in that a game plan is required in order to win. The difference is that in tennis the game plans must often be formulated by the juniors themselves, without the help of a coach or coaching staff. This is why young tennis players must learn to turn their minds on to help them reach their potential best. Most important, they must learn to do this by *themselves*.

The best way to begin planning and adopting game strategies is to scout your opponents. Discover their likes and dislikes and what shots they prefer in different match situations. If you are unable to scout your opponent beforehand, ask someone who might know your opponent's game as many questions as you can relating to his or her play. The information you receive can be a tremendous help in formulating the proper game plan to use against them.

Be prepared with alternative game plans should you find yourself losing in the match. It is important to remember that *you should always change a losing game and never change a winning one*. This is the most basic, but also the most sound, strategic advice I can ever give to you. Before the match ever begins, map out in your mind several game plans in case your first one fails. Plan A, for example, might be your favorite play — baseline rallies — and your opponent's weaknesses — backhand shots and mobility. In this plan, your strategy is to out-rally your opponent from the baseline by placing balls to the backhand side and moving him or her with wider-angled shots. If Plan A should falter and you find yourself behind by a significant margin, another game plan will be needed to try to get yourself back on a winning track. Plan B might be as drastic a change as becoming more aggressive and charging the net, or it might be as subtle as not angling the

ball out as wide during the baseline rallies.

Be flexible in the preparation of your game plans. Your strategies will initially be built around your strengths or the weaknesses of your opponent (or a combination of the two). But be prepared to adopt an entirely different strategy than you've planned if it becomes necessary during the match. Your favorite style of play may not be the correct game to use, or you may discover that your opponent's assumed weaknesses aren't actually so weak. Once you learn to use your mind for strategic planning, you'll be on your way to developing a more advanced game. When a strategy has been devised, stick to it. Don't change it if you're winning and be flexible enough to change it if you're losing.

LEARNING TO READ THE BALL AND YOUR OPPONENTS

Players who have learned to read the ball and their opponents effectively are the ones who always seem to be in the right position to play each shot. They appear to possess an uncanny "court sense" while they're playing. By *anticipating* what the ball will force your opponent to do and by picking up on your opponent's habits, you too will be able to gain valuable foresight to best position yourself each time on court.

Anticipation is no more than instant recall of a previous similar situation. Keep your eye on the ball and watch how your opponent reacts to its varying speeds, bounces, and placements. It can force your opponent into making particular shots. Your awareness of his or her reactions and your retention of this knowledge become valuable stored information in your computer-mind. When these situations occur again, let your mind recall what happened before so that you are prepared for the shots they will probably attempt.

Your opponent has certain habits that should also become stored information. To analyze his habits, look to see where he generally goes on a wide variety of strokes. Maybe he hits most of his forehands crosscourt and likes to hit his backhand down-the-line. The majority of his forehand volleys go down the middle of the court while he attempts to drop volley at the net balls hit to his backhand side. Maybe his overhead smashes all go crosscourt and he comes into the net behind all balls that bounce before the service line. Look for any patterns of play that exist. They can help tip you off as to what you should expect to see in the future.

Watch the way your opponent prepares to strike each ball. Does he line up the same way when he directs the ball crosscourt and down-the-line? Usually you can tell where the ball will go by watching the *shoulders*. If they begin moving early on the swing, look for an early contact or crosscourt hit. If he waits until the ball is closer to the body before swinging, it will probably be a later contact or down-the-line placed shot. Does your opponent step into the shot with his weight and keep the ball in front of the body? Look for a more solid and forceful shot when he does. Or does he lean backward, off-balanced to strike the ball at his side or behind him, taking the pace off the ball and generally sending it higher?

Your opponent's *backswing* offers another clue of what to expect. Full backswings make powerful hits, while shortened swings usually produce softer placed shots. The height of the backswing will also indicate what type of spin might be attempted on the hit. A higher backswing means underspin, while a low backswing can indicate a topspinning shot is coming.

Balls that are hit deep in the opposing court, hit hard or with lots of spin, should indicate your control over the point and allow you to take command of the net. When shots are hit low to their feet or to their weaker stroke it also allows you to take advantage of a weak or defensive reply. However, when your shots land short or land to your opponent's strengths, be prepared for offensive shots coming your way!

Good court sense can be learned and developed by using an alert mind and keen awareness of what the ball and your opponent are doing. You will actually become a much quicker player on court when you learn to position yourself ideally each time by anticipating what will likely occur.

CHOOSING SHOTS INTELLIGENTLY

Raw, young, talented players can often hit a variety of shots but have little sense when it comes to *shot selection*. I have been a witness to this fact in working with many talented juniors over the years. Shot selection is so important that it alone can separate the levels in tennis.

Your mind operates much like a computer. For it to be able to work to your benefit, it must first be turned on, and then it must be programmed. When it has been properly programmed with all the necessary information, you can then play the game more in a state of automatic as your conscious thought will give way to your subconscious belief in them.

To program your shot selection, several factors will need to be taken into account: your court position; the height, speed, and spin of the oncoming ball; the game of your opponent; your own game as well as the varying conditions and situations of the match. To help program your mind for intelligent shot selection use this basic rule of thumb guide:

> Attack short balls, be aggressive on mid-court balls and play defensively balls placed deep to you. Cautiously play low hit balls, aggressively strike waist- to shoulder-height balls, and play defensively balls taken above shoulder-height from the baseline area.

Players who exhibit poor shot selection are the ones who make senseless errors by playing too aggressively on deep and low balls. They play too many high balls offensively from the baseline and miss many opportunities by neglecting to take advantage of short ball placements. If their minds were programmed, when these situations occurred they would know how to react automatically with shots that offered a high percentage rate of success.

Intelligent players don't gamble unreasonably with their shots — only when necessary. They play the game within themselves, using strokes they believe in and can count on. If they make an error, they learn from it and immediately correct it in their minds so they won't continue to repeat it. They automatically select the best shot to play through the use of their computer-minds and in the process avoid making so many unforced and unnecessary errors during the matches they play.

EFFECTIVE SHOT PLAYING

Keep the ball in play, keep it deep and away from your opponent, and hit it to his or her weaknesses. This is a standard strategic formula that should be used as a base to build your winning game plans from.

As your level of play increases, simply keeping the ball in play may not be enough to win matches. The amount of control you have over the ball then becomes an important factor. Your shot placements can make all the difference. Maybe your opponent has good groundstrokes and is able to effectively stay in every rally with you. If you have the ability to hit the ball to him short and deep, high and low, hard and soft, with and without spin, in close and outside, then you will probably be able to discover more weaknesses as well as keep your opponent out of rhythm and guessing what

shot to expect next from you. Remember, ball control ultimately means opponent control, which in turn leads to control of the match.

In a match pitting two players of equal ability, the player who learns to recognize and play the big points well will come out on top every time. I've seen countless matches where two players are evenly matched with the score going to deuce in many games, only to see it end in a lopsided score. There are many big point situations in every match: the first point in every game, all the points when the score is even, thirty-fifteen and fifteen-thirty, as well as all advantage points. Recognizing these points in the matches you play and learning to play high percentage tennis to win the majority of them will certainly make you into a formidable opponent who is very difficult to beat.

The top players in the game all have one thing in common — a *weapon* they can count on. This is usually one favorite shot they feel confident in using, but it can also be a particular style of play, such as serve and volleying or baseline rallying. Since many matches are decided by only a few points, players who have developed a "weapon" are at a definite advantage in these key situations by having the ability to produce effective shots when necessary.

ADAPTING YOUR GAME AS NECESSARY

Rarely will all conditions be perfect when playing a match. So why do so many players practice and prepare as if it were going to be?!

Ideal playing conditions aren't common because it is difficult to have great weather with the perfect temperature and the right amount of sunshine and wind. Tennis balls don't always bounce the same, and opponents won't always hit you all the shots you would like to play.

The best way to practice is to play on a variety of tennis courts with different surfaces to understand the playing characteristics of each. Play in all kinds of weather to know what to expect. Practice playing at night on occasion. Play against a variety of tennis players to prepare yourself against many different styles of play. You will then be best prepared to adapt your game as necessary to the many varying conditions during actual play.

The consistently winning players are prepared to meet and handle the various conditions and situations of each match they play. They understand how to adjust their game when playing in ever-changing weather conditions: hot and humid, cold, windy, drizzling, or cloudy. They are prepared to play against all types of players: left-handers, two-handers, spin shot artists, big powerful hitters, touch players, pushers, and lobbers. They also understand how the court surface they are playing on will affect the bounce of the ball: slower and higher bounce on textured courts (clay, newer hard surface courts, and some synthetic courts); lower and quicker bounce on smooth surfaces (grass, older hard surface courts, some low pile carpet, and slick rubber surfaces).

Sometimes it might be necessary for you to adjust the preparation and timing of your strokes to continue playing a comfortable game. If your control of the ball is ever lost, go back to the basics. Work to get an ideal contact with the ball by setting up your body properly with good footwork for a natural swing at the ball. Lengthen your contact to direct the ball again with control. Speed up your feet and slow down your swing. Analyze the errors taking place so that you can learn from them and make stroke corrections to avoid repeating them.

Most matches are filled with emergency situations. The more experienced players are in control of these situations since they're ready for them. Inexperienced players often find the situations controlling them. Novice players can even be made to feel the entire match is an emergency situation! This is why it is so important to resist the temptation to learn a one-dimensional game. Even though a well-rounded game may take more time to develop, in the long run fewer limitations will mean fewer emergency situations you will have to face. If you have weaknesses and your opponent places the ball to them with regularity, you will constantly find yourself in a crisis. However, if your game has fewer weaknesses and your opponent is unable to exploit any of them, your opponent will probably be the one in the crisis situation!

OPPONENTS PLAY AS WELL AS YOU ALLOW THEM TO

So many tennis players who experience "off" days with their games don't understand why. Most of them can offer 1001 excuses but usually none of them pertain to the opponent they were facing. Although some players' games do change, clever opponents are the usual cause of poor play.

When opponents give you shots you don't like, you are sure to have an "off" day. You also might be having a difficult time in the match simply because you're playing to your opponent's strengths and giving him the shots that are his favorites. This is when you should change a losing game. Analyze your opponent to discover his likes and dislikes. To play the kind of shots that your opponent dislikes might require you to play an entirely different game than you're used to. This is a difficult adjustment for many juniors to make.

Your opponent may have a smooth baseline game with sound strokes that produce few errors. It looks like you are facing a very tough opponent unless you play shots that change his pattern of play. Force him, rush him, pull him out of position, or play different speeds or spins that will change his rhythm and timing. Players who rely on grooved groundstrokes build their game on rhythm and timing. Anything you can do to break this pattern will force them into having an "off" day. This isn't unsportsmanlike conduct; instead, it is the very essence of strategy and tactics in tennis.

If your opponent likes to charge the net, don't allow him to. Beat him to the net first, lob him, or keep the ball deep so that he won't have the opportunity to come in behind the short ball. If you watch closely, you can also discover what stroke your opponent prefers to come to the net behind. Then simply don't allow him the chance to hit that shot by keeping the ball away from that particular stroke.

The top players in the game know that there is no better way to dominate opponents than to beat them at their own game. If you can play to their strengths and still win the points, psychologically they will be beaten with nothing to fall back on. The majority of players should still attempt to defeat their opponents by exploiting their weaknesses. This doesn't mean you should play every shot exclusively to them. Mix up your shots and break your opponents' rhythm and pattern of play with a variety of shots they don't like. Change the pace and direction of your shots, the tempo of the match, and your style of play. Your opponent will never have had such an "off" day in his whole life!

SUMMARY

Be aware of your capabilities and limitations before attempting shots that you are unable to execute. This is the first step to developing your own game style. Then learn to plan and play the game you are capable of to consistently achieve successful results.

The worst strategy in tennis is to hit the yellow ball, yet this seems to be the most common strategy adopted by most juniors. Remember to always change a losing game and never change a winning one. Good court sense can be learned and developed by using an alert mind and a keen awareness of what the ball and your opponent are doing.

Shot selection is often what separates the levels in tennis. Program your computer-mind to react automatically with high percentage tennis. It will help you avoid making so many unforced and unnecessary errors by choosing your shots intelligently. Learn to recognize the big points in every match. Players who play these points well will be victorious in the majority of matches they play. Prepare yourself to make adjustments to your game as necessary in the varying conditions and situations you may face. Rarely will all conditions be perfect, so don't prepare as if they were going to be. *Your opponent always plays as well as you allow him to.* Mix up your shots with a variety of placements that your opponent doesn't like. He may not admit to it, but you'll know the true reason for his "off" day performance!

Chapter 6

MASTERING THE MENTAL GAME

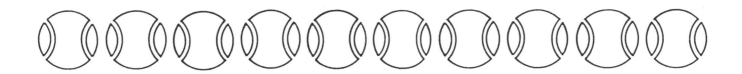

YOU ARE YOUR TOUGHEST OPPONENT

It's easy for players to keep their composure and play a smooth match when everything is going their way, but let something interfere or change the flow of the match in some way and many players lose control of themselves. A simple mistake can set some players "off" while a bad line call or other ill-timed condition can make others lose control.

Self-control, or the ability to retain control over yourself through all situations both good and bad, takes a great deal of mental strength. One of the first signs of a junior player often is the lack of mental discipline (or maturity) on court. Complete control over your emotions in a tennis match is not easy to accomplish, no matter what age you may be. If you want to perform up to your highest ability, however, self-control is a vitally important requirement.

Players in control of themselves won't let losses or poor play affect them. They don't outwardly express their anger and aggression on court because they realize that it will only hinder their play. In the process, they exhibit better sportsmanship and court behavior, not to mention consistent play, with better results.

Many of the great tennis players in the past were known for their "icy," emotionless play. Even though off the court they may have had colorful personalities, on court they performed using their "game face." They were prepared to play in control and weren't going to allow anything or anyone (including themselves) to negatively affect their play.

It's easy for me to relate to this chapter because as a junior I lost to myself more often than anyone ever beat me! In tennis, whoever makes the fewest errors usually wins, and I was the one usually making the errors. It took me a long time to learn to play percentage tennis and to eliminate making so many mistakes. It also took many years of competitive play to discover the secret of self-control and how it could be used to bring out my best play on a regular basis. I was playing against myself for so long — fighting to control on court my thoughts, anger, frustrations, and fears. Not until I learned that I could control my mental discipline was I able to avoid being my own toughest opponent.

Attempt to be at ease with yourself on court. Don't fight with yourself or let distractions control you. They arc probably affecting your opponent as much as they are affecting you, so remain in control and be patient while they affect your opponent instead. Eliminate the negative self-talk and quit dwelling on your past mistakes. Everyone makes errors in the game. Winners, however, analyze their mistakes to learn from them, but refuse to dwell on previous happenings. This is one of the main reasons why they are such tough opponents — they refuse to beat themselves. To win against them, you've got to beat them. They won't hand you the match on a silver platter as many less-disciplined players will.

TURNING "ON" YOUR MIND FOR SUCCESS

Tennis is a mental game. The sport does have its physical demands, but the psychological demands are also great. It's difficult to pinpoint exactly what percentage is physical and what percentage is mental but as the level of play rises, the importance of the mental requirements is clearly greater.

Experienced players use their minds on court. They allow for maximum mental potential by *concentrating* and focusing their minds to the task. They turn their minds "on" to strategic and tactical thinking to avoid playing the game mindlessly. And they instill confidence and belief in themselves by choosing positive thoughts to identify with their play.

Consistently winning players who have successfully advanced their games have done so by learning to concentrate on every hit, no matter who is on the other side of the net. They have discovered that to perform well consistently requires the ability to concentrate well consistently. To play equally well against all levels of players is no easy task. In fact, it's often easier to play well and concentrate better against tougher opponents since minds wander out of boredom or lack of intensity against lesser opponents. Optimum concentration should become your goal every time you take to the courts. It shouldn't matter whether it's a practice match, drill time, lesson, school match, tournament play, or just a hit. By consistently concentrating well on court you will be developing your mind much like you work to develop your strokes. You will then be able to bring out your best play on a regular basis, no matter who your opponent.

Strategic and tactical planning will be formed from your perception, analysis, and thoughts of your opponent and the match. You will probably become much better at spotting weaknesses across the net the longer you play the game and the more experience you acquire. Likewise, you will also become a better thinker on court as your mind develops over time. Learn to analyze your own game as well as that of your opponent each time you play. Tailor your strategies to suit your style of play and the game needed against your opponent. Remember to *think positive*. What's the use of turning on your computer-mind if you are programming it for defeat? Think positive and program yourself for success!

DEVELOPING A WINNING ATTITUDE

Nothing can help your game more than a positive attitude and an enthusiasm for what you are doing. Who is responsible for your attitude? *You* . . . and you alone! Since an attitude is formed by habits of thought, yours can be shaped through discipline over what you are thinking.

The worst problem you'll probably ever face in tennis is a *bad attitude*. Tremendous tennis abilities can be wasted when a bad attitude sets in. It can block out a person's desire to learn, alter the concentration and focus of the mind, and slowly break down a person's self-control. You could even say that your tennis future is decided by what you *think* and *believe*. Think discouraging thoughts and you will be a discouraged tennis player. Think encouraging thoughts and you will be an encouraged and motivated player. What you think about most often will form your attitude. So control what you let yourself think in order to develop your attitude into whatever you desire it to be.

Learn to think positive thoughts and block out those that are negative and self-defeating. Enjoy yourself on court and remember the good shots that you've hit to help ease the pain or errors. "Smile" when you make a mistake. You'll exhibit better sportsmanship and class, not to mention better self-control and mental strength. If you remind yourself of the many mistakes you've made in the match (or of the many problems you may face in life for that matter), your mental game will suffer from it and so will your play.

A winning attitude doesn't mean you should become obsessed with *winning*. It is striving for your best play, giving 100%, and regularly playing up to your potential best. It is committing your mind to the task by channeling all of your energies into the determination to be the best you can be. With willingness, desire, and discipline over your thinking, you can make your attitude into a winning one. You'll be amazed at how such an attitude change can make you into a better player overnight.

RELAXING ON COURT

One way to free yourself from worry on court is simply to *relax*. You don't want to relax your mind, just the muscles in your body. You will discover that most of your worries will stop once your body becomes truly relaxed on court.

The important thing to remember about relaxing is never to force it. It will never come about by trying so hard to relax. Chances are

you'll only create more tension for yourself by thinking so hard about it. It must come effortlessly and easily or it won't come at all.

Tension automatically increases in the body as negative thoughts enter the mind. Anxiety, worry, fear, frustration, and temper can all tighten the muscles in your body and hinder your play. Positive thoughts, on the other hand, calm the mind and allow it to concentrate better. Think positive and relaxed thoughts when you aim to produce positive, relaxed strokes. It's not easy to observe and correct faulty strokes without passing judgment on them, but this is what a mature tennis player does.

Anxiety is often seen in inexperienced players, who are unsure of their strokes and play. Stress itself is not so bad as long as you learn to manage and control it. When not properly managed, stress can affect your body in a number of negative ways. The muscles tense when anxiety enters the mind, which can cause fatigue and injuries. It can also cause many players to "choke." Choking is what athletes call "fear of failure." When a player chokes during a match and misses a shot, the muscles in the body are tense, the heart is racing, the player feels clammy, maybe even nauseated. This is all happening because anxiety is present in the mind.

The first thing you should do if you ever find negative emotions controlling your play is *slow down*. Slow down your walk and your breathing. Take more time between points. Attempt to clear your mind of all unwanted thoughts. Relax your body and recommit your thoughts to the challenge of the match. Breathing a slow breath can help send a signal to the mind telling it that the body is relaxed and back in control.

Advanced players can often be heard "grunting" (exhaling) as they strike the ball. This is to relax their muscles on the hit and

Players often lose their concentration in between points by allowing their eyes to wander. Control your concentration by focusing on your racket at the conclusion of each point. Adjust your strings or simply look at your racket so that your mind will remain on court and not wander off uncontrollably.

lengthen their contact with the ball for maximum control. Be exhaling at contact, their muscles are more relaxed, so their strokes are longer and smoother. Not only will this technique relax your body more, but it will also help you better focus your mind through a controlled breathing technique.

CONTROLLING YOUR FOCUS

One of the most common phrases yelled on a tennis court is "Watch the ball!" This is often the result of players attempting to better focus their minds and concentrate on the match, not necessarily because they are mad at themselves for not visualizing the ball better.

It is true that controlling your eyes on a tennis court can help you control your mind.

Allowing your eyes total freedom can offer the mind too many distractions. The more your vision is focused, the more your mind is focused with intense concentration on what you should be concerned with. When your focus is broad, less attention is paid to the task at hand.

Concentration is the ability to focus in on the here and now. It is freedom from internal and external distractions. Blocking out past and future thoughts helps you better concentrate by "moment-compartmentalizing" your thoughts. Ideally, your focus is on the ball, the point, the match, the moment, the here and now. Concentration is a skill that can be developed through practice. Once you learn to focus your mind better, your attention and concentration will then become more controllable.

A wandering mind will focus nowhere and

too many thoughts will block out your ability to concentrate. Control your thinking so that it will allow you to be a relaxed and confident tennis player. Discipline your mind to stay away from anger, worry, embarrassment, discouragement, guilt, frustration, confusion, depression, panic, or nervousness. Thinking positive thoughts allows you to relax automatically since you feel more confident with yourself. Your concentration will then become easier to hold since your mind is more at ease.

Most junior players tend to be overexcited when playing the game of tennis. They are far too intense and uptight to play their best. Their strokes appear rushed, and their games are racing in an uncontrollable gear. They could probably discover a much higher level of tennis in themselves by simply toning down their intensity or learning to psych themselves down. Everyone has an optimum intensity level at which they perform best. To find the level of intensity that will bring about your best performance you will need to learn to adjust your intensity to find which works best for you.

To tone down your intensity and focus better on what is occurring, slow down your breathing and the pace of your walk. Stop to tie your shoe strings, adjust the strings of your racket, or do some other timely act that will help you gain a few extra moments to relax and adjust your intensity to a more desirable level. Even though giving 100% of yourself is ideal, trying too hard can be self-defeating. Be intense with your play, but at a level you can control and feel comfortable playing at.

BELIEVING IN YOURSELF

Winners see what they *want to happen* while losers fear what *might happen*. The difference in the two is *confidence*. A confident tennis player feels good about himself even when his play is really "off." He has a clear image of his abilities and believes in them.

Confidence in a player can be developed through a conditioning process of practice and belief. It requires positive habits of thought in your mind and in your actions. Learn to *think like a winner*. Visualize and think positive thoughts that you would like to see happen. Block out doubtful thoughts on things that have yet to even occur.

Many young players have trouble believing in themselves and their abilities. The problem is that when they place themselves at a particular level, they will usually remain there until they change the way that they think of themselves. Become a confident player by painting in your mind a good image of your tennis abilities. Regard yourself and your abilities in terms of your *strengths*. Don't forget your weaknesses when it's time to improve them, but don't measure your tennis game strictly by them.

A winner is someone who believes he will win. He believes this until the final point of the match has been played. If he finds himself behind in the match, he has the ability to surge ahead through his strong conviction and belief in himself as well as his determination in refusing to accept defeat.

Developing your confidence will probably begin on the practice court with strokes you can always count on and with positive mental thoughts of yourself and your actions. Even though reliable strokes will help you lay the foundation of your game, most players could become much better if only they would put their minds to it. The average player is too insecure with faults and weaknesses to think beyond them. They unknowingly spend most of their time programming their minds for defeat.

A self-confident person is a believer. It is actually belief that instills confidence in the player. If you believe that you are the player with the ability to excel, chances are you will do just that. However, when you doubt yourself and your abilities, your play will become self-defeating.

So many tennis matches are won or lost before they ever begin because of self-doubt or over-confidence. The important thing to remember is that your opponent is only as good as he plays that day. Learn to put your opponent's reputation, whether it's good or bad, out of your mind. Play the shots that your opponent hits that day and forget about his name. Don't become "psyched-out" before the match ever begins. Likewise, don't let over-confidence ruin your chance of victory.

THE AMAZING RESULTS OF MENTAL STRENGTH

Great unexplained feats have occurred when a person has channeled all of her thoughts and energy into a single task. This repeatedly happens in emergency situations where someone is in desperate need of help and a person lacking the necessary physical requirements is able to come to their aid in a miraculous fashion. When a tree, a car, or some other large and heavy object is crushing someone, it would seem impossible to save them when the object weighs 1000 pounds or more. But it has been achieved many times by people just like you and me. When the mind is keenly focused with all of its energy directed into a single task, you can achieve many more things in life than you probably are aware of.

In the beginning ranks of tennis, the mental aspects play a very small part of the game since the main focus is on learning the strokes and developing techniques. However, as the levels increase, the mental game plays an ever-increasing role. *Maturity* has a lot to do with the strength of one's mental capacity, and this is the reason many juniors fail to tap into their

mental resources. Girls have the advantage of maturing earlier than boys, which is why you often see more younger girls than boys doing well on the pro circuit.

Henry Ford used to say, "Whether you think you can or you can't, you're probably right." Words can really be quite powerful. When you say something, your mind believes it. This is why it is so important to choose what words you say to yourself and what thoughts you dwell on. Self-talk is something all people do. Some like to talk out loud to themselves, while others prefer to keep their words only in their minds.

The "power of suggestion" can be your worst enemy or your dearest friend, depending on how disciplined your thinking is. Miss a first serve — just for a split second think that you might double fault — and sure enough, you will! This is the result of undisciplined thinking. However, suggest to yourself that you will win the match and watch the determination and desire to win magnify within yourself.

"Always act as if it were impossible to fail," says Norman Vincent Peale in his book, *The Amazing Results of Positive Thinking*. Winners are too concerned with winning to worry about losing. They won't give up until the last point has been played, even when they're behind by a large margin. Their minds are determined and motivated with a strong will and desire for victory. It is their mental strength that makes them into tough competitors. By refusing to accept defeat, these determined players will usually be the victors in the matches they play.

SUMMARY

Junior tennis players often lack mental discipline and maturity on court. Many have yet to fully understand and realize the importance of self-control. You will always be your own toughest opponent until you learn to discipline your mind and control your emotions. Optimum concentration should be your goal every time you take to the courts. By consistently concentrating well, you will be developing your mind much like you work to develop your strokes.

Your tennis future will probably be decided by what you think and believe. Nothing can help your game more than a positive attitude and enthusiasm for what you are doing. If you ever lose control of yourself on court, relax. Slow down your walk, your breathing, and your strokes to gain your control back. Focus your vision only on what you should be concerned with and keep your intensity at a level you can control.

Become a confident player by believing in yourself and your tennis abilities. Visualize and think positive thoughts you would like to see happen and avoid doubtful thoughts on things that have yet to even occur. Whether you think you can or you can't, you're probably right, so discipline your thinking to become the determined player who believes he can. The most determined player in a tennis match is the usual victor when two players of similar ability levels are competing. The difference in their mental strength is often the deciding factor.

Chapter 7

TOURNAMENT PLAY AND COMPETITION

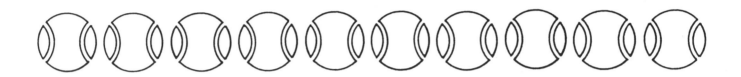

ARE YOU READY FOR COMPETITION?

Let me begin by saying that there is no ideal age for starting to play competitive tennis. All tennis players — juniors, adults, and seniors alike — should only compete when they are ready, are eager, and feel naturally inspired to play competitively. It should be a natural process, and they shouldn't compete unless they *feel ready and want to*!

The worst thing that can happen to you when you decide to compete is that you may lose. One-half of all tennis players competing around the world will lose. That is because each match produces only one winner (two winners in doubles). Some players are able to accept losses better than others. A loss represents *defeat* to some players, while it becomes a *challenge* and motivates others. When players don't feel compelled to compete and aren't truly eager and ready for competition, several losses can actually be so demeaning and defeating that some will even quit the game for good! Competition in individual sports such as tennis can be devastating and should not be overlooked. However, when players are naturally prepared mentally along with having the

proper perspective, competitive tennis can offer terrific growth potential and be a lot of fun!

Unfortunately, success in our society is often measured by wins and losses. Winning isn't everything though. I'm not saying losing is great fun but usually the real losers in life are the ones who never try anything! Everyone in tennis has had their share of losses, including the top-ranked professionals. It takes time to gain experience in this sport and in the process of growing, it is necessary to lose some matches so you can learn from them and continue forward.

I always tell my young tournament playing juniors the true story of my first taste of competition. The first tournament I ever entered was held at a local city park in Florida, and I was scheduled to play the top seed, the number one ranked junior in Alabama in his age division. He beat me like a drum (6-0, 6-0), without blinking an eye or losing a game. Was I defeated? No way! I was so motivated and inspired that all I wanted to do was improve. For the next two years I played every tournament I could enter, losing early in most of them but gaining valuable experience along the way. I met the same top-ranked junior almost two years to the date later, this time on his home courts in Alabama, and beat him in two easy sets! It took me a little time and a lot of losses, but I proved something to myself that day . . . when you love this great game and enjoy competing in it, you're sure to improve your game and better yourself along the way!

LOCAL LEAGUES, TEAMS, AND LADDERS

For many, the best initial exposure to competitive tennis can be found in various tennis activities in your local area. Tennis/racket clubs, city park tennis facilities, and even many schools offer organized play for juniors. These are often in the form of leagues, teams, challenge ladders, and other activities that involve organized practices and matchplay. For more information about junior activities in your area, contact your area school, local tennis or racquet club, local tennis association, or local city park recreation facility. If you are unable to find any answers at these locations, contact your Sectional Association of the USTA. Their phone number and address is listed at the end of this chapter. They are directly involved in promoting junior tennis at the local level and can give you information about the programs offered in your area.

HOW TO ENTER TOURNAMENTS

There are several types of junior tennis tournaments: non-sanctioned (or local events), USTA sanctioned (sectional ranking), USTA Satellite (non-ranking), National, and International. Local tournaments, which are non-sanctioned, are often the best way to experience tournament play for the first time. They usually offer girls' and boys' divisions in the twelve-, fourteen-, sixteen-, and eighteen-and-under age categories for both singles and doubles competition. Players sign up and play in a division according to their age (i.e., a fourteen-year-old boy plays in the boys' fourteen-and-under division and a fifteen-year-old girl plays in the girls' sixteen-and-under division).

Some local tournaments set their divisions by ability levels instead of age. Typically the divisions in these tournaments are Beginner, Advanced Beginner, Intermediate, Advanced Intermediate, and Advanced. If this is the format, boys and girls of varying ages are often grouped together and will compete with one another.

If you have enjoyed competing in non-sanctioned local tournaments and are anxious to test your skills at a higher level, you may want to enter sanctioned tournaments. Sanctioned tournaments are officially recognized by the United States Tennis Association. There are specific guidelines that sanctioned tournaments must follow as well as guidelines that participants must follow to compete in these events. The divisions for these tournaments will be boys' and girls' twelve-, fourteen-, sixteen-, and eighteen-and-under singles and doubles, unless otherwise specified. Participants must be a member of the USTA or purchase a membership card at the start of the tournament. The current USTA junior membership is $10.00 per year. Consult the tournament director to discover which age division you will be eligible to compete in, since your birthday may require you to play up into the next higher division.

Most sanctioned tournaments qualify for rankings, but Satellite events do not. These tournaments are for non-ranked players and offer an easier transition for players competing in local events to step into USTA sanctioned play without the pressures of competing for a sectional ranking.

National and International tournaments

STANDARD ENTRY FORM

(Print or type all information)

Name of Tournament _____ Telephone _____

Address _____ Date of Birth _____

City _____ State _____ Zip _____

USTA# _____ Expiration Date _____

I apply for entry into the following events:

_____ Partner _____

_____ Partner _____

_____ Partner _____

Entry fee must accompany this form $_____. Please attach a copy of current year's record.

_____ _____
ENTRANT   DATE

_____ _____
PARENT OR GUARDIAN (If entrant is a minor)   DATE

are for the elite or top-ranked players in the section and nation. There is usually a selecting committee or some other means of consideration to determine which players to invite to compete in these prestigious events. If you are very successful in USTA sanctioned tournament play, contact your USTA sectional office for further information on National and International tournament eligibility.

The best way to enter tournaments is to fill out an entry form and mail or hand-carry the entry to the tournament site *yourself*. I've often seen parents and coaches do this for their children, but I believe that if youngsters have the true desire to compete, they should take the initiative to register themselves in the tournament. For the very young player, aged twelve and under, this may not apply, but separating the child's desire to compete from their parents' desire for them to compete can easily be seen during tournament sign-ups. Filling out the entry and seeing that it reaches the tournament desk in time teaches them responsibility, independence, and how to manage and understand deadlines and procedures. These are all terrific qualities to instill in children at an early age and will usually stay with them for life.

If you are unable to obtain an entry form for the tournament you wish to enter, most events will accept the above standard entry form. Be sure to fill out the entry blank completely and enclose the necessary entry fee. If the tournament offers doubles and you plan on playing, most require that you sign up by the singles' deadline, while others allow doubles' sign-ups the first day of the tournament. Be sure to check when the doubles' sign-up deadline is and make sure your partner is eligible to compete in the age division in which you are entering.

Most tournaments will not accept telephone entries, and those events that do will usually not guarantee them. To insure that entries reach tournament site by the deadline, they should be completed and mailed in early. Be sure to attach a copy of your recent results if you are interested in being seeded or placed in the draw as one of the top players according to your playing record.

PREPARING FOR TOURNAMENT PLAY

When preparing to compete in tournaments, players should aim to establish a routine for themselves. Routines are habits or regular procedures that tournament players perform prior to matchplay. They help them feel comfortable, confident, and ready to perform to the best of their ability.

When should you arrive for the match? What do you do when you get to the tournament site? What should you eat and how much sleep should you get the night before? During the day of the tournament, what should you eat and drink? What is the best way to prepare mentally and physically? What equipment and accessories will you need? These are but a few of the questions you will need to answer in order to begin establishing a suitable routine.

I'd like to offer some general guidelines for you to consider, which might prove helpful in finding your routine. Call the tournament site the day before the tournament begins to find out your scheduled match time. On the day you are scheduled to play, arrive forty-five minutes to an hour early, checking in with the tournament desk upon arrival. To break a sweat and relieve a little of your nervous tension, try to get in some early practice time on the practice courts available. Try to hit a variety of strokes during your practice and at the conclusion, play a few points out as you would in the match. If no practice courts are available, go for a short, light jog around the facility or jump rope for several minutes. Stretch to relax the muscles in your body after you have finished the warm-up. Players who stretch their cold bodies before the warm-up are risking injury.

Get plenty of sleep the night before to feel rested and ready on match day. Fill your system up with carbohydrates (pasta is ideal) and drink lots of water. This will help to provide plenty of stored energy throughout the tournament and guard against dehydration. Focus on your goals the night before, planning how you will play. By painting a positive mental picture of yourself you will be preparing your mind for optimum results.

You should always allow enough time before each match for the food that you've eaten to digest, say one and a half to two hours. This will help you avoid feeling bloated and immobile on the court during play. On match days stick to light, low fat foods like fruits, vegetables, pasta and breads, and other foods high in complex carbohydrates. Drink plenty of liquids before and during each match, even if you're not thirsty. Water is always the best liquid to consume and should be with you at all times during tournament play.

Try to steal some quiet time for yourself before each match. Look for an isolated spot to go to alone, and relax and focus before play. Attempt to block out everything around you and think about your game plans, your goals, and how you see yourself playing the match. This quiet period is the ideal time to calm yourself and become relaxed while collecting your energy and focusing your attention on the match. Players who simply show up at the tournament site and socialize with friends until the time they play are missing a key element in pre-match preparations — preparing the mind for matchplay.

Check your racket and equipment before the tournament. Make sure that the grip, strings, and frame are all in good order. If possible, bring two (or more) rackets that are comparable and strung similarly. The additional rackets are a form of insurance if something should break or happen to your first racket during matchplay. Bring wristbands, extra shirts, towels, and socks, and don't forget a water jug. Extra spending money for snacks and meals will also be important unless you plan on bringing your own.

THE TOURNAMENT DRAW

After the tournament deadline has passed and all entries have been received, the tournament committee makes the draw for each division of play. They will place in the draw certain players who have the best playing record by *seeding* them according to ability. This is so they will not meet and play against each other early in the tournament. One seed is allowed for every four competitors in the division or a major fraction thereof. After the seeded players have been determined and placed, *byes* will be put into the draw sheet to round out evenly the number of players needed to form the draw. With twenty-four competitors playing in a division, for example, eight lines on the thirty-two draw sheet will have a bye. The eight players scheduled to play against the bye will not have a first round match and will automatically proceed to the second round. After the seeds and byes are placed on the draw sheet, the remaining players will be drawn randomly and placed on the sheet in a "blind draw" format, sight unseen to insure fairness for all placements.

Some tournaments are single elimination, while others offer a first round consolation or feed-in consolation bracket. The purpose of the consolation bracket is to allow the losing

32 PLACE DRAW

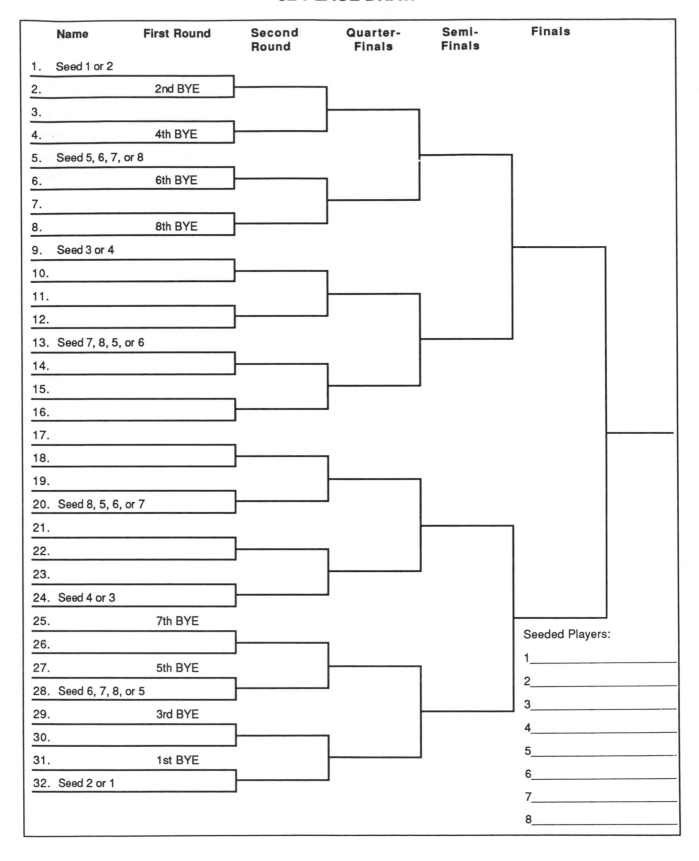

Name	First Round	Second Round	Quarter-Finals	Semi-Finals	Finals

1. Seed 1 or 2
2. 2nd BYE
3.
4. 4th BYE
5. Seed 5, 6, 7, or 8
6. 6th BYE
7.
8. 8th BYE
9. Seed 3 or 4
10.
11.
12.
13. Seed 7, 8, 5, or 6
14.
15.
16.
17.
18.
19.
20. Seed 8, 5, 6, or 7
21.
22.
23.
24. Seed 4 or 3
25. 7th BYE
26.
27. 5th BYE
28. Seed 6, 7, 8, or 5
29. 3rd BYE
30.
31. 1st BYE
32. Seed 2 or 1

Seeded Players:

1 _____
2 _____
3 _____
4 _____
5 _____
6 _____
7 _____
8 _____

64 PLACE DRAW

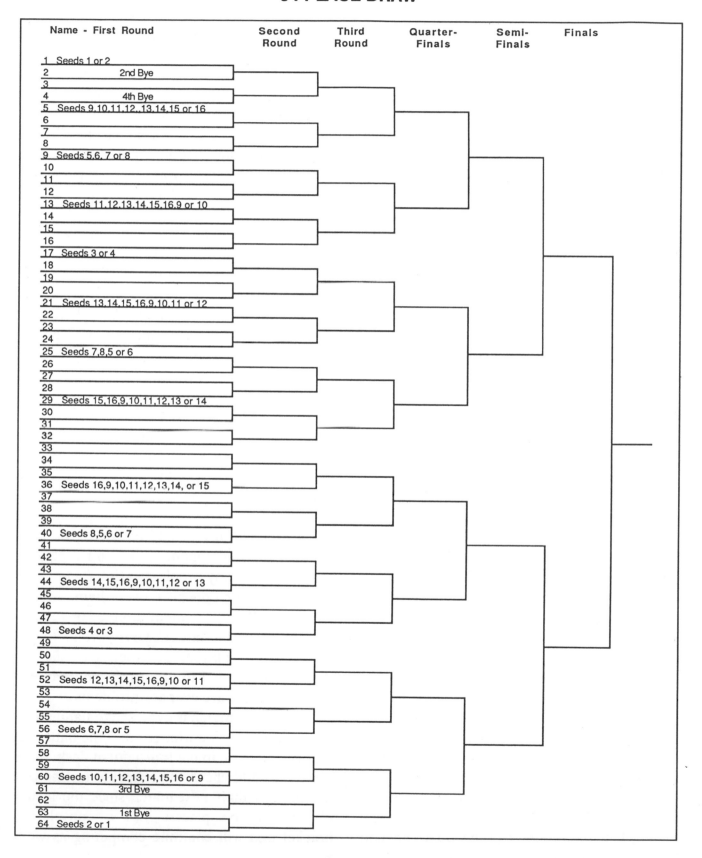

players of the main draw a chance to continue playing. The first round consolation bracket is for only those who have lost in the first round of the main draw. This makes sure everyone has at least a chance to play two matches in the tournament. Feed-in consolation brackets allow losers through the quarterfinals (or final eight) of the main draw a chance to continue competing in what is sometimes called the "back draw" or consolation event.

How many participants have entered your division in the tournament will determine the size draw you will be competing in. The standard size draw of thirty-two or sixty-four may not apply if the tournament is very small or extremely large. If your division is a small one, it may only be a four, eight, or sixteen size draw. If it has a very large field, it may have up to 128 players competing. If only four have entered your division, the tournament committee may decide to hold a *round-robin competition*, in which every player must play every other person in the draw.

UNDERSTANDING AND ENJOYING TOURNAMENT MATCHPLAY

Several officials will most likely be on hand throughout the tournament to see that the event runs smoothly. The tournament director, referee, umpire, line umpires, and tournament desk committee are the officials you should be familiar with.

The *tournament director* is in charge overall of running the tournament. If you have a problem, it should be addressed to either the tournament director or the tournament referee for resolution. The *referee* is the official in charge of the rules and procedures of tournament play. The *umpire* (if one is assigned to your court) is the official in charge of a specific match. The *line umpires* (if they are assigned to

your court) are the officials positioned around the perimeter of the court who rule on particular lines they are assigned. The *tournament desk committee* is often made up of volunteers who check in the players and give out court assignments, as well as collect the scores at the conclusion of each match.

Check in with the tournament desk when it is time for your scheduled match and remain close by until they call your name to play. Pick up the balls and proceed to your assigned court when your match is called to play. Players generally are allowed only a five minute warm-up, so use your time wisely. Hit a variety of shots that you intend to use in the match, and try to feel comfortable and confident with your shots. Watch your opponent throughout the warm-up, looking to see which shots he or she likes and which ones he or she doesn't. This will help you to devise strategies and game plans to use throughout the match.

Since most junior tournaments do not have umpires or line umpires, you should know and understand all rules of the game. Inexperienced tournament players often get taken advantage of on the court when they are unfamiliar with the rules. Be a good sport throughout the match and above all, be considerate to your opponent and those playing around you. If any problems arise, *do not ever argue with your opponent* over them, simply search out the tournament director or referee for resolution. Do not ask your parents to get involved. The players, not their parents, are the ones who need to talk to the tournament officials if there are ever any problems.

When the match is over, shake hands with your opponent. The winner takes the balls and reports the score to the tournament desk. Both players should check the schedule to find out the time of their next match since the losing player may be placed into a consolation bracket and will continue competing as well.

Players will generally be required to play up to two singles matches and one doubles match each day of the tournament. A reasonable rest period, however, should always be given between matches.

If you feel nervous or pressured playing in tournaments, communicate your feelings to your parents or coach. You must understand that it is not uncommon to feel that way; even the top playing professionals have attested to feeling "butterflies" in their stomach before big matches. It is the joy of competing that makes tournament tennis so much fun. It is the struggle of getting there, not just the success, that inspires so many to love the challenge of this great game. Competing in the sport of tennis does bring many rewards for young, developing adults. It provides travel opportunities and teaches goal-setting, sportsmanship, respect for rules, patience, persistence, work ethics, and positive thinking. It also helps to develop well-rounded individuals with good self-images and self-esteem.

Tournament tennis provides a healthy environment to expose youngsters to as they build mutual friendships and develop a good attitude towards interacting with others. It also is a way for families to share in a sport and grow closer together in the process.

GETTING A RANKING

To earn a ranking, players must compete in their age category in a specified number of USTA sanctioned tournaments. Usually the minimum number of tournaments required to be eligible for a district or sectional ranking is anywhere from three to seven. Check with your sectional offices for more information on the requirements if you are interested in pursuing a ranking.

Players are usually responsible for getting their tournament playing record to the ranking committee for ranking consideration. Your ranking will be based on your matchplay results — wins, losses, exposure (or quality of opponents), and comparative scores in sanctioned tournaments during the ranking year. A *tentative ranking sheet* is usually published several times throughout the year in each section to assist tournament directors with proper seeding placements in their draws. The final rankings for each USTA section are published in the Sectional Yearbook and can also be seen in the annual USTA yearbook.

Rankings provide short- and long-term goals for many aspiring young players. Even though a ranking is not a measure of a player's skill, it does say a lot about a player's tournament results. Interested players should plan out their calendar year. You should be selective and pick out which and how many tournaments to play. Players should generally not participate in more than ten to twelve tournaments a year. "Burn-out" has been known to occur in players who simply overdo it. This is one of the main reasons that the USTA has eliminated the National twelve-and-under age tournaments for rankings. The pressure on this young age group was causing many highly-ranked players to drop out of the sport.

Competition and *experience* is what players competing in the younger age groups (twelve and fourteen) should be playing for, not rankings. Tournament play should remain fun, while rankings are more downplayed, especially with these younger age groups.

There are many benefits to striving for and achieving rankings. Being ranked can help you get better draw placements in future tournaments that you play. It can also help you qualify for major sectional events. Highly ranked players have the opportunity to compete on intersectional teams, attend special training camps, and become eligible for national teams.

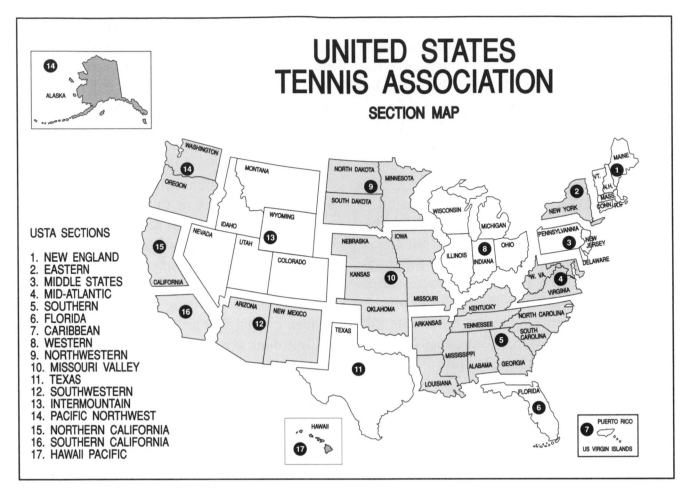

USTA sectional map.

Tennis scholarships are also available at most colleges and universities, and players with rankings usually receive first consideration.

SECTIONAL ASSOCIATIONS OF THE USTA

Section Offices

For tournament schedules or other sectional USTA information, please contact your appropriate section:

Caribbean Tennis Association
P.O. Box 40456, Minillas Station
Santurce, PR 00940
(809) 765-3182

Eastern Tennis Association
202 Mamaroneck Avenue
White Plains, NY 10601
(914) 652-3533

Florida Tennis Association
801 N.E. 167th Street, Suite 301
North Miami Beach, FL 33162
(305) 652-2866

Hawaii Pacific Tennis Association
3558 Waialae Avenue #207
Honolulu, HI 96816
(808) 735-3008

Intermountain Tennis Association
1201 S. Parker Road #102
Denver, CO 80231
(303) 695-4117

Mid Atlantic Tennis Association
P.O. Drawer F
Springfield, VA 22151
(703) 321-9045

Middle States Tennis Association
580 Shoemaker Road
King of Prussia, PA 19406
(215) 768-4040

Missouri Valley Tennis Association
722 Walnut, Suite 1
Kansas City, MO 64106
(816) 556-0777

New England Lawn Tennis Association
P.O. Box 587
Needham Heights, MA 02194
(617) 964-2030

Northern California Tennis Association
1350 Loop Road, Suite 200
Alameda, CA 94501
(415) 748-7373

Northwestern Tennis Association
5525 Cedar Lake Road
St. Louis Park, MN 55416
(612) 546-0709

Pacific Northwestern Tennis Association
10175 SW Barbur Blvd., Unit 306B
Portland, OR 97219
(503) 245-3048

Southern California Tennis Association
P.O. Box 240015
Los Angeles, CA 90024
(213) 208-3838

Southern Tennis Association
200 Sandy Springs Place, Suite 200
Atlanta, GA 30328
(404) 257-1297

Southwestern Tennis Association
2164 East Broadway, Suite 235
Tempe, AZ 85282
(602) 921-8964

Texas Tennis Association
2111 Dickson
Austin, TX 78704
(512) 443-1334

Western Tennis Association
2242 Olympic Street
Springfield, OH 45503
(513) 390-2740

SUMMARY

Competitive tennis play should be a natural process in which players compete only when they feel ready, eager, and naturally inspired to do so. For those who are ready for it, competitive tennis can offer terrific growth potential and a lot of fun! There are probably several ongoing tennis activities in your local area, which you can join to experience matchplay such as leagues, teams, and ladders, as well as tournaments to compete in.

When preparing to compete in tournaments and other competitions, players should aim to establish a *routine* for themselves. You will want to be comfortable, confident, and ready to perform to the best of your ability. Since most junior tournaments do not have umpires or line umpires, you should know and understand all rules of the game. Be a good sport when playing competitively, and above all, be considerate to your opponent and those playing around you. If any problems arise on court, do not argue with your opponent or get your parents or spectators involved. Simply search out the tournament director or referee for resolution.

It is the joy of competing that makes tournament tennis so much fun. To earn a ranking, players must compete in their age category in a specified number of USTA sanctioned tournaments. Rankings provide short- and long-term goals for many aspiring young players. However, players competing in the younger age category (twelves and fourteens) should compete for the fun and experience, not focusing on higher rankings. The USTA Sectional Association offices can give you tournament schedules and information about the programs offered in your area (see listing of section offices).

Chapter 8

INSTRUCTION AND COACHING

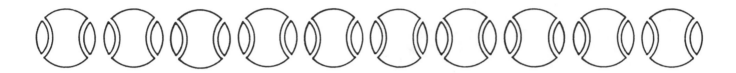

FINDING THE RIGHT PRO

Very few players have progressed very far or achieved much success in the sport of tennis without the help of a good instructor or coach. Finding the right tennis professional is important, and it can be as easy (or as difficult) as finding the right attorney, doctor, or dentist. Ask around to hear who others might recommend. A good referral is often the best way to discover the right pro for you.

When you do find a teaching professional who is recommended and held in high esteem, go and talk with him or her. It wouldn't hurt if you also talked with their students (and parents of the students). You might even want to watch him or her give a lesson. There are a variety of tennis teaching professionals in the business, just as there are a variety of doctors. You wouldn't let every doctor perform surgery on you, just as I'm sure you wouldn't want every tennis-teaching pro making changes to your game.

The first thing to look for is a teaching professional's *certification*. The world's oldest and largest association for teaching professionals is the United States Professional Tennis Association (USPTA). To qualify as a USPTA member, applicants must pass a thorough written exam and score high marks on an on-court playing test and instruction lesson exam. Teachers are then rated as a "Professional 1," "Professional 2," or "Professional 3" according to their ability level, score, and experience teaching the game. Another organization that certifies its members is the United States Professional Tennis Registry (USPTR). It also requires rigorous testing to certify prospective members. Find out if your professional is certified and what his or her rating is. It can often tell you a lot about the credibility and knowledge of the person.

The prospective professional should be easy to talk to. Communication skills are just as important as having the knowledge of the game. The pro should be easily understandable without offering too much bull. When he or she has a passion for the game, it is often transcended into a positive, encouraging, and motivating teaching style. Any tennis teaching professional who is not positive and encouraging in his or her instruction should not be considered. You want a caring friend, someone to motivate and inspire you to reach your best, not to bring you and your game down.

How involved is this professional in local, regional, and national events within the tennis industry? Does he or she stay current with the latest teaching methods, looking for ways to continue learning and improving? This may

The communication skills of your tennis teaching professional are as important as the knowledge they have of the game. He or she should have a positive, encouraging, and motivating teaching style.

not seem so important to a beginner level player, but to advanced-level and tournament-level juniors, the advanced knowledge of the instructor is crucial. Does he or she have contacts with sporting goods manufacturers for tennis equipment? Does he or she have contacts with colleges and universities? Juniors who have achieved success in the sport and are ranked in their section can often qualify to receive tennis equipment for free or at a special reduced rate. Teaching professionals with good contacts with manufacturers are often the best reference source for sponsorship equipment. They can also be responsible for helping to save many families tens of thousands of dollars by helping young graduates go to college on tennis scholarships. There are approximately 1500 colleges and universities that have tennis programs and offer tennis scholarships. Any help and guidance that a teaching professional can offer could prove invaluable in the future.

Having a good record as a player won't necessarily make the person a good tennis teacher. In teaching advanced juniors, however, it does help that the teacher can relate to the pressures of competition and understand the feeling of advanced tournament play. It can also help the teacher gain respect when he or she is able to trade strokes and successfully play out competitive points with top students.

The best teaching professionals don't just develop strokes or games, they develop *players*. They teach the mental, physical, and tactical skills necessary to play one's best. They don't teach systems, they teach individuals in a flexible way. And their students become independent players with the intelligence to correct their own mistakes and the maturity to motivate and discipline themselves. They realize that teaching professionals can only guide and instruct; the actual performance on court will be up to the player alone.

GETTING MORE FROM YOUR LESSONS

The most successful tennis lessons are often decided by the *pupil*, not necessarily the teacher. It is very important to have a caring, knowledgeable, and enthusiastic tennis instructor, but it is usually the *attitude* and *attention span* of the student that will dictate how well the lesson is understood.

To get the most from your lesson time, *arrive early*. Warm up to get the blood flowing and muscles loose. Hit a variety of shots much the same as you would to warm up for a match. This way you won't have to waste precious and valuable instructional time getting your strokes "grooved." You'll discover you will be more fresh, focused, and eager to begin after a light workout as opposed to going on the court cold to begin your lesson after stepping out of a car (or off your bicycle).

It should be a privilege for you to take tennis lessons. Don't waste your parent's money or your teacher's time going into lessons with the wrong attitude. Be open and willing to learn, asking questions if the instructions aren't clear or easily understood. You have the right to understand clearly every point your instructor is trying to make, so don't be shy. It's your time on the court with the teacher and it will be up to *you* to make sure the advice you are receiving makes sense.

Be patient with your progress in learning the game of tennis. Champions aren't born

overnight and you wouldn't want them to be. There would be too much competition for you! Understand that everyone makes mistakes in tennis. You have the advantage in that a professional will help you to understand *why* you are making mistakes and to learn *how* to correct them when you do. Correcting mistakes is what learning the game is all about, so don't get impatient or angry with yourself when you make an error.

It is often what you do with what you've learned that matters most. There is no substitute for practice, so take what you've learned in your lessons and work to develop it into a part of your game on the practice court. It is sometimes difficult to remember all of the key points in each lesson; that's why it is recommended to always take notes. Write down the important items the pro mentioned that you need to work on, along with any homework or practice advice suggested. (The Appendix provides a section entitled "lesson notes," which you can use to log your lessons.)

If you prepare properly for your lessons — arriving early and in the right frame of mind, being open and eager to learn — but still don't feel that your instructor is helping to advance your game, seek the advice of another pro. Patients get second opinions from other doctors, and it's not uncommon for students to try other tennis professionals either. Sometimes varying opinions and viewpoints can help you gain a new perspective on your game that you wouldn't be able to get with just one instructor. Or it may be that it helps to solidify the confidence and trust you have for your first instructor by realizing he or she is still the best teacher for you.

Relax during your lessons and let the time be enjoyable. You are there to learn, but that doesn't mean you shouldn't enjoy yourself. Your teacher may be tough on you, but he or she is probably only trying to bring out your

In large classes (6 or more), it's often difficult for students to receive personalized instruction. Group instruction, however, can offer the most fun way for juniors to learn the game.

best. If your teacher is too much of a "push-over" or "nice person," you may not respect him or her enough to work hard enough to play up to your ability. Just like in school, the teachers who are the best on the tennis court are usually tough, but fair and enthusiastic. They will be the memorable ones and will probably be the ones that you most admire and respect.

PRIVATE VERSUS GROUP INSTRUCTION

Some people perform best in a group while others peak in privacy. When learning the game, you will probably have your choice of taking either private, semi-private, or group instructions, depending on which instructor you choose and the junior program offered.

If you can afford the higher cost, private instruction provides the most intensified individual attention and is the quickest way to develop players. By working one on one, the teacher is able to help accelerate the learning process by offering closely guided instruction. The pupil is given 100% of the pro's attention

and focus, and the student is able to work on isolated problems or personal preferences.

Semi-private lessons can be beneficial when two players with similar ability levels and compatible goals take lessons together. The small number on court with the professional still insures individual instruction to each, at a lower cost. The instructor is able to spend roughly 50% of his or her time with each student, with enough time to still work on isolated problems with each. It helps if the students are friends, and it's nice when the two can be hitting partners to practice together what they've learned in their lessons.

Group instruction, like semi-private, is fine as long as the individuals have similar ability levels and are compatible on court. The smaller the group, naturally the more personalized the instruction will be for each. When juniors are well-organized and kept active, group instruction can offer the most fun means of learning the game, especially when the experience is shared by others and friendships are developed on court.

Beginning-level juniors often find group instruction the best way to learn the basics of the game. They are able to watch others in the group make mistakes and realize that they too make errors and miss shots. It makes them feel better when they see others playing the game at their own level. They can also meet other young potential practice partners and friends. The intense individual instruction is often diminished in group instruction, which eases the pressures of learning and makes tennis more fun and enjoyable.

SHOULD YOU ATTEND A TENNIS CAMP?

Just as there are a variety of tennis teachers, there are also a large number of tennis camps to choose from. If you are thinking of attending one, there are several important factors you may want to consider before enrolling:

❏ Who are the instructors? Are they all certified professionals? (Some camps sell themselves by using the Director's name, but use inexperienced instructors to teach the program.)

❏ What is the ratio of students to pros? (It shouldn't exceed 6:1; 4:1 is ideal.)

❏ What does the program consist of? (It should be compatible with your goals, commitments, and desires.)

❏ What are the level of players who attend? (It is important that you fit in and feel comfortable.)

❏ Does the camp offer other sports? Is there free time? (This depends on your interest.)

❏ What is the philosophy of the camp? (Very important!)

Most tennis camps offer intense instructional programs geared around the teaching philosophy of the director, head professional, or founder of the camp. Some stress physical

conditioning including a run either at the beginning or at the end of the day and a weight workout (or some other physical activity) as a part of the tennis program. Other camps believe in drilling and will have students hitting thousands of balls each day. Still others believe in match practice and will schedule competitions into the program. Some even take their students to area tournaments during their stay. There are camps that stress the basics and fundamentals, and there are camps that teach more advanced bio-mechanical methods.

It is important that you first decide what it is you hope to gain from attending a tennis camp. Once you know what you are looking for, you will then be better prepared to search out the right camp for you. If an intense, competitive, tournament-level camp is what you're after, you won't get your money's worth at one that is geared to the beginner and teaches the basics. And if you're an intermediate-level player who is just beginning to taste competitive tennis, a very intense and advanced one may turn you off from the sport entirely.

When chosen correctly, tennis camps offer players many benefits. They offer a variety of coaches to learn from and plenty of compatible players to befriend and practice with. You will usually have the opportunity to play a lot of tennis, get great workouts, and be in better shape. Chances are you'll become a better player and have a lot of fun in the process!

THE PLAYER/PARENT/COACH RELATIONSHIP

When learning the game of tennis, it's not easy to always feel good about yourself when you're missing shots and losing matches, being corrected by your instructor, and being counseled and guided by your parents all the while. A delicate *balance* is required by the "support

Most tennis camps offer instructional programs geared to the teaching philosophy of the director or founder of the camp.

team" of parents and coaches to build the player's confidence, keep the pressure off, and emphasize the fun!

Providing a positive support group should be the primary concern of those around the player. If the parents or the coach of the young player are too demanding or controlling, the player is made to feel like a "puppet" with everyone else pulling the strings. Even though a support team is ideal, tennis is still an individual sport since it will ultimately be the player who will be performing on court ... *alone.*

The parents and coaches of the players should avoid too much of a good thing. Support in large doses can mean "overkill" that suffocates young players with undue stress and pressure. Remember that tennis should above all be fun! The goals and expectations of what the child wants to achieve in tennis must come from within, not from those around him. When the student begins playing for others, burnout is probable. Even though most young players are not naturally self-motivated, parents must be cautious in their approach when attempting to stimulate motivation.

When communication breaks down, a "Bermuda Triangle" can develop between the player, parents, and coach. This is the reason that open communication channels must exist between all parties for a winning support team to work. Parents and coaches must learn to listen to the player both on and off the court. The communication must be able to flow both ways for it to be effective.

When the coach's values are in line with the family's and open communication exists between all, the youngster feels the love and support of the harmonious group. As long as helpful praise and positive guidance are provided, the player is able to perform up to her ability level without feeling the pressure of meeting anyone else's expectations but hers alone. And in all probability, she will feel more motivated to excel because the support group has shown *belief* in her, which is so vitally important in the development of self-confidence and self-esteem.

SUMMARY

Search for a teaching professional who is certified and highly recommended. Shy away from teachers whose instruction is anything less than *positive* and *encouraging*. It will often be *you*, the student, whose preparations, attitude, and attention span will dictate how well your tennis lessons improve your game. Remember, it is usually what you do with what you've learned that matters most, so take notes and practice after each lesson.

Whether you take private or group lessons, learn to relax and enjoy your instructional time. Understand that everyone makes mistakes in tennis, and that you have the benefit of a professional helping you learn *why* you are making mistakes and teaching you *how* to cor-

rect them when you do. If you are thinking of going to a tennis camp, decide first what it is you hope to gain from attending, then search out the right camp for you. When chosen correctly, tennis camps can offer youngsters many benefits.

Parents and coaches should aim to offer a support team to build the player's confidence, keep the pressure off, and emphasize the fun. When helpful praise and positive guidance are provided, players perform best because the group has shown belief in them without the pressures associated with expectations.

Chapter 9

PARENTAL INVOLVEMENT

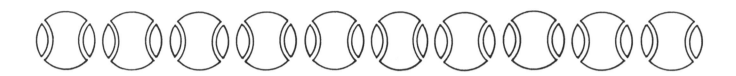

POSITIVE PARENTS VERSUS PROBLEM PARENTS

One of the toughest jobs on the face of this earth has to be parenting. Not only is being a parent a full-time plus around-the-clock job, it also happens to be an "art form" that continually requires a balancing act for the best method since there is no guaranteed formula for success.

A key ingredient to positive tennis parenting is learning to give unconditionally to children. When you expect something in return (i.e., wins), your money's worth from your financial investment in the sport, or even appreciation for the vast amount of time and effort you're spending, you're just giving conditionally. You're really expecting something in return. Parents who instead learn to unconditionally provide their children with every opportunity in the sport, and encourage and support them along the way, realize that's really all they are able to do — provide them with a positive experience. When they lose sight of this fact, the pressures and expectations become too great, which causes many youngsters to "burn out" and drop out of the sport.

It would be extremely difficult for a top young player to emerge today without the help and support of a parent or parents. There is,

however, a big difference between being a *positive parent* and being a *problem parent*. Problem parents become so involved that they feel they, too, are playing the matches. You can often witness these parents at junior tournament sites. They're the ones who come up to the junior tournament desk and ask what time "we" play! I've got news for these people, you aren't going to play, only your son or daughter is!

Communication is so important to understanding your child. Learn to offer positive advice to get back positive feedback. Avoid criticizing in favor of praising. Listen to what they have to say. Maybe it's not "cool" for you to watch their matches, or you make them nervous by being courtside. Does your child see frustration or anger on your face or hear it in your voice when discussing his or her tennis play? Getting angry with children or taking away their privileges for sub-par performances can have many long-term negative effects and should be avoided. Try instead to offer your shoulder and caring ear to them. Chris Evert says that one of the greatest things her father taught her was that it was O.K. to lose. Since the pressure was taken off at an early age, she was able to enjoy competing in the sport, knowing that her family was behind her providing unconditional love and support.

Should you coach your own child?

SHOULD YOU COACH YOUR OWN CHILD?

The question "Should you coach your own child?" raises an issue with no clearly defined answer. Since parents are usually the ones who know their children best, the initial response by many parents is that they are the most uniquely qualified to coach their son or daughter in the sport of tennis. Sometimes this is true, but not always. Several important questions must be addressed before this important issue can be accurately determined.

Can you be objective? Do you possess the necessary skills to be a qualified teacher — knowledge, perception, and communication? Are you patient and understanding with your child? Can you motivate, inspire, and gain the respect of your child on the court? Do you have a good parent-child relationship to begin with? Do you openly communicate with your child? Are you athletic enough?

The old saying "families that play together, stay together" is often true, but when parents begin coaching their children the relationships that develop aren't always "rosy." The better the initial relationship between the player and the parent, the better the chance the duo has in making it work. It depends mostly on the communication the two have to begin with.

Parents who would like to play a larger role in the development of their child's tennis skills should first soak up as much knowledge as they can. Learn the rules of the game and understand the basic strokes, the fundamentals, the strategies and tactics of the game, and the physical and mental demands the sport makes on its players. Start subscribing to all available tennis publications and read every tennis book you can get your hands on. Begin making televised tennis and local tennis events and tournaments a part of your schedule if you don't already do so.

Once you have gained a vast amount of knowledge and feel competent enough to offer your son or daughter advice, take a look around your area. Is there a qualified teaching professional who has more knowledge and experience than you do? Most certified professionals have not only passed rigorous tests to earn their teaching certifications but they also take part in continuing education, which keeps them up to date on the latest teaching techniques. If there isn't anyone in your area more qualified than you to teach your child, be prepared to stay current on teaching trends and the latest advances in tennis technology. Your child's tennis future will depend on it. If you have decided that you are most qualified to teach your child, plan your lessons so that each will have a purpose. Organize your instructional time so that progressive steps will be used to develop your objective. Your student will either be developing good or bad habits, and it will be up to you to distinguish between the two. Make sure that your child understands her strengths and weaknesses. Everyone makes mistakes in tennis, and it will be important that you share with them *why* they made the error when they do. Instill belief and confidence in them by being patient when they miss shots. Analyze their play without being *judgmental*. This is sometimes difficult for parents — to be an objective coach for their children.

Good tennis teachers use touch, visual, and auditory cues in their instructions. They are also enthusiastic in their approach and strive to keep the game fun in the process. They build players up — not down — and work to develop a positive teaching style.

If you are open in communicating with your child both on and off the court, you will probably be able to sense if your child wants you for a tennis instructor or not. My advice is don't push to make it work if it's not going to, and stop teaching when learning isn't taking place. It's so much more important that your parental relationship remains strong and intact than straining it if a poor coach-student relationship begins to develop between the two of you. If you are fortunate enough to be able to coach your son or daughter, you can have the best of both worlds, and save yourself a fair amount of money in the process!

TEACHING SELF-MOTIVATION

There is a fine line between *encouraging* and *pushing*, just like there is between *supporting* and *motivating*. Parents and coaches alike must learn to encourage and support, but not be the impetus that pushes and motivates. This must come from the child, and from the child alone.

One of the keys to developing self-motivation in a child is to get them to want it for themselves. If others want them to play the game far worse than they do, the "burning, insatiable desire" for the game won't be present. This form of inspiration creates only a small flame within them, and it's usually a matter of time before the fire dies down and their flame is "burned-out."

Self-motivation is generally developed in children at a very early age. It becomes more difficult to develop at a later age, but competing in individual sports can often help. There are many advantages for youngsters playing team sports but self-motivation is usually better-developed in individual ones. In team sports a coach tells the players when, what, and how to practice and develops the strategies both offensively and defensively for each game. In tennis, only one person and one person alone can decide the outcome of each match, the player himself. This is the reason why self-motivation is so important in individual sports. I always tell my students, "I'm only a teacher. The choice is yours in what you do with the information I'm sharing with you. You will get back what you put into it, since you're the only one in control of where you are going."

Let the young players determine what their own goals in tennis will be. This can help to shape and formulate their desire for playing the game. If they are only driven by the aspirations their parents or coaches have set forth, their motivation is sure to be short-lived. Most players lose motivation when it's not fun anymore. It usually isn't fun when pressures are being applied either internally or externally. Parents can help relieve many of the pressures by providing love, concern, and support, along with helping to bring back the enjoyment the child has for playing the game.

Hard work has never killed anyone, but pushing a child to play the game of tennis can often prove detrimental. I was extremely fortunate to have parents who let me discover the love for the game on my own. I can count on one hand the number of times in my life my parents pushed me to practice or to play a competitive match. I was self-motivated; I didn't need to be pushed or driven to play. I wanted it for myself and for myself alone. For this, I am most thankful because I now realize that only I can control where I'm going in life and it's up to me to get there. I'm not a passenger looking to be driven somewhere; I'm the driver and I know where I'm going!

HANDLING BEHAVIOR PROBLEMS

No one likes to see young players misbehaving on the tennis court . . . especially when it happens to be their own sons or daughters! It's never a pretty sight. You can almost feel the frustration and anger of the youngsters as they lose control of themselves on the court. But what is a parent to do?

It is a fact that players who lose control of themselves and their emotions on court will certainly compete at a lesser ability level. The tension that is created inside of them restricts the muscles in their body, which inhibits smooth and flowing strokes from taking place, while an angry, frustrated mind is filled with negative and self-defeating thoughts. This valuable information should be shared with all young players so they will realize that emotional control is an important element of reaching one's potential best.

It's not always easy to compete in a sport at an early age when there are so many demands to be *mature*. Even though sometimes children just have to be children, it is the way they are brought up by their parents that often dictates just how disciplined they are on the court. When five-time Wimbledon Champion Bjorn Borg threw his racket on court at an early age, his parents took his racket away for a month! For those of you who remember Bjorn Borg, throughout his illustrious career he was always a model of emotional control and gentlemanly conduct on court, thanks in large part to his parents and the discipline they instilled in him early on.

By nature, children like discipline. They like structure in their lives but they won't tolerate weak authority. Parents whose aim is to curb intolerable on-court behavior should set the rules and then be prepared to stick by them. No match can be too important and no incident too small to bend or break the rules set forth. The rules will be the rules, and it will be important that your child realize that the rules will be what governs her on-court conduct.

I've always found that most juniors are too

Players who lose control of themselves and their emotions on court will certainly compete at a lesser ability level.

"keyed-up" or over-intense when playing the game. This can often lead to uncontrollable behavior without their even knowing it. I teach my students to be relaxed during play and to slow down to gain control. I also stress that only they can be in control of themselves and their thoughts and emotions on court, and that their control can either positively or negatively affect the outcome of the match. I tell my students to "act like a professional on court and you'll play like one!" It helps them to develop self-discipline and self-control while they are building character and class in themselves.

I've pulled several young players from the court before, and I've given my fair share of warnings as a tournament director at junior events, but I haven't seen as many parents be as firm with their kids over the years. It's hard

to "lay down the law" years later if they have been so soft with them all of their lives. Parents (and coaches) can definitely help them learn to develop their control on court, but not without *rules and guidelines*. Once they are established, it is up to the youngster to abide by them and up to the parents and/or coach to make sure that they do.

UNDERSTANDING THE IDEAL PERFORMANCE STATE OF YOUR CHILD

Special demands come with being an athlete. Pressure to excel and achieve success comes from family, friends, and within. This is in addition to the many other pressures which come

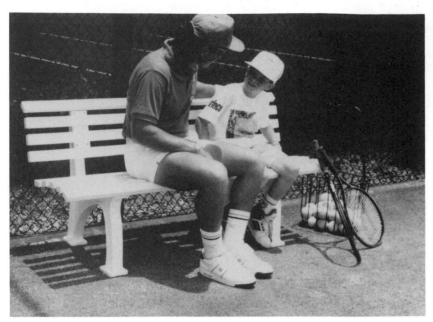

Teach your child that it's okay to lose. Success in the sport shouldn't only be measured in terms of wins or losses.

with adolescence. Sometimes it can all be over-whelming or too much for children to handle.

Playing up to one's highest ability level is no easy task, especially on a regular basis. Everything must be just right for it all to "click" into place and allow the player to switch into the highest gear and play the game in automatic. Your body must be relaxed with the mind sharply alert, in focus, and in control. You must also be a confident player who believes in yourself and your ability. You must discipline your thinking to foster positive thoughts along with a positive attitude. You must possess a keen desire to play your best and at an intensity level that reaches optimum output. This deep state of concentration allows you to play the game in automatic as your conscious thoughts give way to your subconscious belief in yourself.

Parents who understand what it takes to reach and play at the ideal performance state are best prepared to be a part of helping their kids reach their potential best. Reducing pressure will certainly help to increase their enjoyment in playing the sport and should be practiced at all times. It is also important to build their confidence by showing belief in

them and teaching them to believe in themselves. The practice court is usually where confidence is developed in players, along with match experience, which is gained over time. Help them understand that they have control over their thoughts and actions on court. Teach them *self-discipline* and *self-control* and it will play a big part in helping them perform at their highest level on a regular basis.

GUIDING YOUR CHILD TO SUCCESS

When success in the sport is measured strictly in terms of wins or losses, everyone can be the loser. The child feels the pressure to win and will often misbehave on court to vent the frustrations he is feeling. Cheating may even take place and love for the sport often diminishes when the pressure to compete, excel, and win becomes the primary focus for playing the game.

Parents can burn out their star tennis prodigy and turn him away from a lifetime sport of enjoyment when winning is placed as the top priority. Values and morals can be lost, friendships and even families can suffer when the driven desire for achievement becomes too great in the sport. Tennis is such a positive sport with so much to offer youngsters. It is a lifetime sport and a great character-builder for the young adult.

Playing the game should be a positive and rewarding experience that they enjoy and that helps to prepare them for the successes of everyday life. Help your children grow in many ways as players and as people in a sport they can have for life. But if they should happen to fail, let them fall back on something — your love and support. The important thing to remember is not to offer too much of a good thing by smothering them with all of your love and support!

The very fact that you're reading this book shows that you are an involved and interested parent. That's great. Remain genuinely interested in the activities they are involved in (like tennis), win them over to your side, and then instill in them important values like time management, goal setting, responsibility, and commitments. Then step back and realize, tennis is just a game. Don't make it greater than it really is . . . let them enjoy it!

SUMMARY

One of the toughest jobs on the face of the earth has to be parenting. A positive tennis parent learns to give *unconditionally* and eases the pressures by not expecting something in return from the child. The decision to coach your own child or not isn't an easy one. If you are open in your communication on and off the court you will probably be able to sense if your child wants you for a tennis instructor or not. Don't push to make it work if it's not going to, but, if you are fortunate enough to be able to coach your son or daughter, you can save yourself a fair amount of money in the process!

The key to developing self-motivation is to get youngsters to want it for themselves. Most players lose motivation when it's not fun anymore. Emotional control is an important element in playing one's best. Children should learn and understand this. Children like discipline but won't tolerate weak authority. Set on-court conduct rules and guidelines for kids with behavioral problems and then be prepared to stick by them.

Playing up to one's highest ability level on a regular basis is no easy task. Parents should understand this and try to help their child learn to relax and be confident, disciplined, and in focus while playing. Teach them that only they can control these things on court, through self-discipline and self-control. Success shouldn't be measured in terms of wins and losses with your child. You are providing them a positive and rewarding experience that they should enjoy. You may have to step back sometimes and realize just that . . . tennis is a game that, above all, should be enjoyed!

Chapter 10

SUCCESSFUL TRAINING HABITS

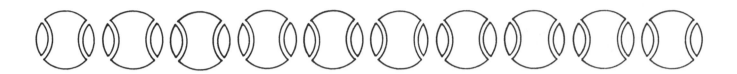

PRACTICE WITH A PURPOSE

How many times have you gone out on the tennis court alone or with a friend just to hit balls? Every time you practice or play you will be developing either good habits or bad habits — the choice is yours. That is why it is so important that you use your practice time wisely and plan your practices accordingly.

Aimless hitting produces aimless play. Balls that are directed all over the court without targets in mind are really just uncontrollable shots being practiced. The mind isn't used with this form of tennis, so what results is not only aimless play, it's *mindless* play too! When players choose to practice this way, just hitting the yellow ball without targets or use of the mind, they are really choosing to develop bad habits instead of good ones.

Focused players are usually driven by a vision. They know what it is they are going after and channel all of their energies into "going for it." You probably won't see these players hitting aimlessly or mindlessly because they are concentrated each time they walk on court. They are going somewhere with their tennis, and they realize that in order to get there they must use their practice time to develop their games and improve their play. They are motivated and disciplined because they have be-

come "goal-oriented."

Most youngsters haven't learned or enjoyed the benefits of goal setting. This is why individual sports such as tennis can be so beneficial in the development of young adults. When goals are set, young players learn to focus on a task. And when they achieve goals, it helps to establish confidence and self-esteem as well as gratification, a sense of accomplishment, and pride.

All tennis players, from the beginner to the advanced, should have goals set for themselves. Obviously the goals or aspirations of the players will vary with each level and individual, but it is important that every player set a direction to head for in the sport. When setting goals remember to be *specific* and *realistic*. Goals are not necessarily dreams, but there is nothing wrong with "thinking big" when establishing your long-term goals. Think on where you would like to be three months, six months, and a year from now with your tennis game. These will be your short-term goals. Your medium-range goals will be from one year to two years from now, while your long-term goals may be as far away as three to five years.

Your short-term goals will provide the initial steps required to take you where you want to go with your tennis game. Once these are established, you will begin to have a better idea

—117—

Drill practice helps to groove strokes—to make them consistent and develop confidence in them.

A practice wall or backboard can provide practical ways for players to groove their strokes if they are without a partner.

as to what you will need to accomplish in your practice time to achieve them. For example, a player is number six on her high school team and would like to make it into the line-up, or top five positions, by the start of the season, which is three months away. She now has motivation in her practices because she is on a quest to make it into the starting team. If she were specific in setting her goals, she would analyze her game and determine which aspect or strokes need additional improvement. Her practice time could then be spent developing that part of her game.

Players who haven't established goals for themselves often lose interest in practice. Practice time should be exciting, challenging, and fun! You are setting out to accomplish something; to achieve your goals. It helps to think of your target goals often to keep the interest high and desire keen within you. Be prepared to change your goals every so often as needed to keep them current and realistic.

Everyone makes mistakes in tennis, but learning not to repeat them is what makes great players. Realize *what* you are doing and *why* you are doing it when training your game. Learn to see yourself and correct your own mistakes by asking "why" when errors are made. Players who learn to turn their minds "on" and think on their own while on court are sure to avoid the pitfall of playing the game mindlessly in the future.

Ball machines are great practice aids because they are probably the most consistent opponent you will ever face!

DEVELOPING CONSISTENCY

Consistency is what makes champions. Chris Evert played in fifty-six Grand Slam Tournaments throughout her illustrious career and reached at least the semi-finals in fifty-two of them! I think she summed it up best when she said "I wasn't a fluke. I didn't have three good years and then two bad years." She was most proud of her consistent reign at the top as she was ranked in the top four in the world for a span of eighteen years.

Reaching your best playing level is ideal but if you can do it consistently, what more can you ask of yourself? To aim for consistent results with your game, begin by establishing consistent habits. Players who play the game within themselves, that is, the game they know

they are capable of, develop strokes they can count on in practice. You won't see them hitting shots with a low percentage chance of success because they have built their games on reliable strokes that are consistently played.

Drilling is an ideal way to "groove" strokes — to make them consistent and develop your confidence in them. Many players avoid dull drill practice in favor of the excitement of point-playing. While matchplay and point-play are also important, nothing can help to develop your game's consistency more than establishing good practice habits, which includes drilling.

There are literally thousands of drills that can be used. You should seek the advice of your local teaching professional to get advice on which drills would be best suited for your particular needs and game. Start collecting a supply of used tennis balls and search for a practice partner who won't be bored drilling with you. It shouldn't matter what the playing level of your partner is. It isn't important *who* is on the court with you; your aim is to play your best no matter who is across the net.

To establish a rhythm with your strokes, get your feet moving! *Footwork* is often the cause of inconsistent stroke making. Once your feet are lining you up properly for each shot, take aim for a target that is well above the net and within the lines on the opposite side of the court. Give yourself a "safety margin" to help reduce the risk of errors and bring high percentage success to your game. A rhythmic swing flows smoothly and with good length at the contact for the best control of the ball. Relax your body and direct each shot with a target in mind. You will be practicing with a purpose and developing a consistent game at the same time!

PRACTICE AIDS

In addition to a supply of used tennis balls and a court to hit them into, there are several ways you can still practice your strokes without a partner.

A wall, backboard, side of a building, or rebound net can all be used for the practical purpose of grooving tennis strokes. Players stand in front of the backdrop and hit balls into it. This can be repeated as the balls rebound.

Ball machines are excellent practice partners if you don't mind getting beaten! They are one of the most consistent opponents you will ever face and are great tools for developing stroke consistency. Set the machine up on the opposite side of the court. It can then be set to direct the ball anywhere you would like. Highly recommended for all strokes (except the serve).

There are several rebound devices on the market that allow players to practice their strokes alone. Most operate like a "tether ball," which helps to save time from chasing the ball.

QUALITY, NOT QUANTITY

The time you spend on the court practicing your strokes and training your game should be time well spent. Since you are developing either good or bad habits each time you walk on the court, it is of utmost importance that *quality* of time be stressed, and not the quantity of time.

My philosophy is that I don't think you should ever practice unless you feel like it! If you get used to playing when you really don't have the desire, you will develop the bad habit of playing the game with a lesser intensity level. Your sub-par performances will habitually become the norm if you let it. If, on the other hand, you only practice when you feel 100% like it, your attitude and keen desire will help you reach your best more often.

Just showing up, going through the motions, and putting in your court time won't guarantee your tennis game success. What did you learn during your practice time? What did you specifically work on? What did you develop, accomplish, or improve? To stay on a forward moving track requires you to get back what you're putting into your game, but what you're putting into it is not time, it's effort.

In practice, no ball should ever be considered "out." Get into the habit of running every ball down . . . even learn to *enjoy* running for them! This will keep you intense and motivated during practice time. It will also help you realize that you can reach more balls on court than you probably give yourself credit for.

The best time to stop practicing is just before you feel your intensity and desire begin to

The way you practice is generally the way you will play. Learn to be as concentrated and intense in practice as you desire to be during important matchplay.

slip. This will depend on your age and maturity level along with your ability to concentrate. It's better to stop while good habits are still being developed than to let bad habits creep into your game.

A short amount of practice time well spent (i.e., one hour) could do more for a player's game than two to three times as much if improperly used. Have a plan for your time and practice with a purpose. Only practice when you completely feel like it. Try to learn every time you play and work to develop or improve aspects of your game during practice. You will get back what you're putting into your game, so if it's success and improvement you're after, learn to put more quality time and effort into your training schedule.

PRACTICE AS YOU PLAY

When was the last time you let the ball bounce *twice* on your side of the court while playing a match? You probably gave it your all to run it down before the second bounce. How about during practices? Have you always given the same concern for double bounces during practices as you do when playing matches?

The way you practice is usually the way you will play. Your concentration, intensity, total effort, and desire are all determining factors in developing your game and your strokes into the unique player you are. Since a significant portion of your total tennis time is probably being spent on the practice court, it is imperative that you learn to practice the way you would like to play.

Do you talk while hitting tennis balls in practice? Do you keep your eyes focused on the court or do you often look around off the court to see what is happening around you? Do you run all balls down on one bounce? Do you keep your feet moving and line up for each shot with the same precision in practice as you

Every time you practice or play you will be developing good habits or bad habits, the choice is yours. Since good footwork is so important in tennis, short jumprope sessions prior to playing can warm you up and prepare you for quicker on-court movements.

do during matchplay? Do you put the same amount of effort and energy into winning points in practice? Do all of your hits have targets? Do you practice positive thinking and belief? Do you work on your consistency? Do you attempt to reach your highest level of play on a regular basis during practices?

Don't let boredom set in with your practices; learn to be *creative*. Use different drills, change your practice plan, or even change your partner if necessary. Work on different strokes or develop new ones. A winning attitude is just as important as a winning backhand, and yours can be developed by learning to love the challenge of learning!

Players who learn how to play the big points well are sure to experience success in the sport. In practice, test your abilities to meet the stress and pressure of key point situations. The more comfortable you can become at performing well at these intense moments, the more confident a player you will be.

Your training habits will make you or they will break you. It's just that simple. To be the consistent, confident player that you desire to be will require you to give your all in practice as well as in matches. Establish goals and plans

to give yourself direction during practices. Be as concentrated and intense in practice as you want to be during important matchplay. Channel your energy into a high-quality effort. After all, what more can you ask of yourself than giving it your all? If you're not currently giving it your all, however, look to change your training habits. Your success depends on it!

FIT FOR TENNIS

Ivan Lendl and Martina Navratilova have changed the game of tennis into a sport that is much more "physical." They have established themselves atop the world of tennis by training to be in the best physical shape possible. While both continue to put in long hours each day on the practice court, they have utilized their off-court time to benefit their tennis play as well. Lendl likes to mix cross-training and biking in with his weight-training, while Navratilova prefers basketball and track work in addition to her time spent in the gym lifting weights. Both of these great champions feel they deserve to win. They have put in the time and effort to believe in themselves and their abilities.

Many players think that simply playing tennis will make them fit. To play your best, however, will require that you get *fit* to play, not *play* to get fit. For advanced-level players, total physical training is the ideal way to reach your potential best. Through training, Dr. Jack Groppel, Chairman of the Sports Science Committee of the USTA, has stated that, "Players can increase their explosiveness by up to 20% (which is a lot) as well as their cardiovascular system which becomes crucial in long matches."

Up until age ten or eleven, boys and girls are physically the same. After puberty occurs, the gap begins to widen between the two. The only difference at early ages appears to be the "throwing motion," which is more of a technique than it is a physical attribute. As players mature into young adults their bodies change into the compositions listed below:

Male	Female
45% muscle	36% muscle
15% bone	12% bone
3% essential fat	12% essential fat
12% storage fat	15% storage fat
25% remainder of tissue	25% remainder of tissue

(Note the differences in muscle and fat)

As the bodies are growing and changing in young adults, the physical training methods that young tennis players employ are crucial. The old adage "no pain, no gain" is no longer true. A growing number of tennis injuries are being seen developing in players from the junior ranks all the way up through the veteran professionals on tour. Aaron Krickstein, one of the youngest male players ever to emerge on the world tennis scene, has suffered two stress fractures in his left foot, one in his right foot, a strained left knee, a stress fracture in his left leg, and a strained ligament in his right elbow! The hard court surface play, the year-round sport, and the power game that has emerged have all contributed to increased injuries in the game.

As tennis becomes a more physically demanding sport, the players who wish to compete must become more concerned with getting themselves physically fit. It should be noted that players with different styles need to train differently. Racing towards the net to end the point quickly requires the use of different muscle groups than the person who remains on the baseline and strives for longer rallies to win the point. In the 1988 U.S. Open Tennis Tournament, there was a big contrast noted between the men's and women's finals. Take a look below:

1988 U.S. Open Men's Final

Ivan Lendl versus Mats Wilander

59% of the points ended in less than 10 seconds
22% of the points ended between 10-20 seconds
19% of the points lasted more than 20 seconds
average point played: 12.2 seconds
average rest between points: 28.3 seconds
total points played: 325
total match time: 4 hours, 54 minutes

1988 U.S. Open Women's Final

Steffi Graf versus Gabriela Sabatini

62% of the points ended in less than 10 seconds
25% of the points ended between 10-20 seconds
13% of the points lasted more than 20 seconds
average point played: 10.8 seconds
average rest between points: 16.2 seconds
total points played: 161
total match time: 1 hour, 41 minutes

(Note the difference in total points played and total match time.)

Your training habits can make you or they can break you. Cross-training such as biking, running, or other sports can help build strength and endurance.

35% of most match time is spent playing, while 65% is time spent between points. This is why the mental game is so important in tennis! When two players of equal ability compete, the average point on clay court lasts 10 seconds, while on hard courts the average point lasts 5.2 seconds. The average distance run per stroke is 4 meters (approximately 13 feet) while the average directional change required is four times per point. This is important data to consider when developing a fitness program for tennis. The first footstep in tennis cannot be slow. Explosive speed is required in tennis, not long distance speed. The Swedes utilize a training system called "Fartlek" training to develop speed in tennis players. Players jog to get their heart rates up, then sprint for 30 yards, then return to a jog for a short period, then spring backwards for 30 yards, return to a jog, then sprint sideways for 30 yards, etc. This helps to build quick speed in players while helping to develop their agility.

Variety in your fitness training can help to keep staleness from setting in. Mix strength, endurance, and agility into your program. When weight-training is practiced, several cautionary points should be remembered: 1) Train, don't strain, 2) the key to training is moderation, 3) optimize, don't attempt to maximize. Technique is so very important in weightlifting. This is why inexperienced youngsters should always have a monitor with them to teach them the proper use of equipment. The goal should be to develop a solid strength base that is symmetrical (the entire body, not just an isolated area). Flexibility is also important in strength training because the more flexible a muscle/tendon is, the stronger it can become.

Your diet alone can't make you win matches, but a bad one can negatively affect your play. A good diet consists of high quality fuel (food) for your muscles to burn. Complex carbohydrates are the best source of energy. Protein is necessary for growth and repair of muscles and bones, but it takes longer to digest than carbohydrates. This is why (as a rule of thumb) tennis players should: 1) eat more fruits, vegetables, whole grains, and pasta, 2) eat less red meat, 3) drink lots of water.

Inactive people need six glasses of water or other fluid a day. As activity increases, fluid consumption must also increase. When you lose 2% of body weight in water, you lose reaction time and judgment. Nothing works faster than cool water into the system for replenishing lost fluids and nothing works better than plain, simple water for replacing lost electrolytes.

Being fit to play tennis requires a commitment on your part, both physical and mental. Being physically fit not only develops strength, quickness, agility, and endurance, it also helps to increase self-confidence and shape your attitude into one of belief. You must believe that you deserve to win to have the confidence in your self to be able to achieve it. Make it a sin to lose matches because of physical inabilities, and you will be preparing yourself for the physical challenges of playing your best. If you strive for excellence but neglect to develop a total physical training plan, be prepared for injuries, tired play, and balls you can't reach on court!

PLANNING WHEN TO PEAK

The hot topic in tennis today is sport science exercise physiology and the developing program of *periodization*. Periodization is a long-term training plan designed to control the intensity, volume, and frequency of training and competition to optimize the chances for peak performance at desired times.

Periodization was begun in the late 1920's to 1930's by the Russians and has been widely accepted in other sports such as track and field, swimming, weightlifting, baseball, and football. In the late 1980's this systematically designed training program reached the sport of tennis, and it is predicted that in the 1990's and beyond it will change the way tennis players train to compete.

Sports psychologist Dr. Jim Loehr and biomechanic expert Dr. Jack Groppel have used periodization to help players like Michael Chang and top-ranked junior members of the USTA national team develop schedules for tournament training and peaking. *Peaking* is a phase in training when performance is maximized. It involves physiological, mental, and psychological preparation to reach your best at certain times of the year. No two individuals will be exactly the same since it all depends on tournament schedules, level of ability, and conditioning.

The periodization training schedule works in four phases: preparation, pre-competitive, competitive, and rest. The competitive phase is the peak time when players want to play their best. Depending on the level of the player, this would be the important tournaments, matches, or events throughout any twelve month calendar year when the best results are desired. The important thing to note is that players cannot physically or mentally reach their heightened best more than three to four times in one twelve month period, and for no longer than three weeks in any period.

The *preparation* phase lasts five to six weeks and involves building strength and endurance. On court, players should concentrate on high-volume drilling and low-intensity play. Off court, cross training is encouraged with players playing basketball, soccer, swimming, etc. as well as weight-training to develop strength. Players can build up their cardiovascular system and level of fitness as well as make any technical or tactical changes to their games.

The *pre-competitive* phase runs from three to five weeks and approximates competitive play as much as possible. The training focuses on strength and power, anaerobic endurance and speed. The volume (or amount of tennis play) during this period can be decreased, but the intensity at which the game is played should increase significantly. The training during this period is more tennis-specific and should include competitive match practice.

The *competitive* phase should last two to three weeks but should occur no more than three to four times a year. During this period the player is at a high level of peak performance. Trying to peak beyond this period of time increases the risk of overtraining and reduces the chance of competitive success. Players should reduce the volume and increase the intensity of workout to feel rested with a high level of energy and motivation with low levels of stress. Drilling during this period should be short and explosive with decreased activity in off-court training to maintain, rather than build, strength.

The final phase is the *rest* period, which is from one to three weeks. Players are encouraged to take a break from tennis but still maintain a level of fitness. Training should be low in volume and in intensity and can incorporate cross training activities such as running, biking, or other sports play.

Since tennis is a sport without an off-season, players should decide when they want to peak and when they want to rest and recover. There has to be time to develop one's game or to work on incorporating some new change or aspect into one's play during the year. Players can choose several tournaments that are less important and use these as developmental tournaments throughout the year. If you are a serious competitor, consult your local certified teaching professional for guidance in designing a personal periodization training schedule. It will help put you in control of when to play your best tennis.

SUMMARY

Aimless hitting produces aimless play. Players who establish goals for themselves are more driven by a vision. They are motivated and disciplined and usually practice with a purpose (and play that way as well). *Consistency* is what makes champions. To aim for consistent results with your game, begin by establishing consistent habits during practice time. Drilling is an excellent way to groove your strokes, build reliable shots that can be consistently played, and develop confidence in your shot-making abilities.

You will get back what you put into your tennis game. If it's success and improvement you're after, learn to put 100% of your intensity, concentration, and effort into your training schedule. The way you practice is generally the way you will play. Your training habits will make you or break you; the choice is yours, since only you are in control of your practice time.

For advanced-level juniors, total physical training is the ideal way to reach your potential best. Tennis has become a physically demanding sport, and those who wish to compete at a high level must become more concerned with getting physically fit. Players should mix strength, endurance, and agility into their program, along with explosive speed. Serious junior competitors should consider establishing a personal periodization training schedule. It will help put them in control of when to peak and play their best throughout the year.

Chapter 11

THE GAME OF DOUBLES

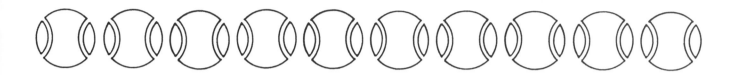

THE DOUBLES DIFFERENCE

Doubles is a game that is often neglected by junior players. Most club level adults prefer the game of doubles, which is probably the most popular form of club tennis played today. Most junior players, on the other hand, tend to overlook doubles play. Fewer juniors are playing doubles in tournaments even though in school team competitions, doubles matches count the same towards the win as singles matches do. It's really a shame that more juniors aren't playing doubles since the game can be the most enjoyable form of tennis played!

To play this game well, you must first come to understand that *doubles is not singles*. There are really very few similarities in the two. The court is 9 feet wider on either side of the net, thanks to the addition of the alleys, and four participate in doubles while two players go at it in singles play. The game of doubles also requires a much larger arsenal of strokes such the lob, volley, half volley, approach shot, and chip-shot among others. This is why many junior players have found that good doubles play is more difficult to achieve than singles.

The game of doubles requires *teamwork* between the two to work together to accomplish a similar task. This means that the players must be mature enough to work together as one, to communicate, and to understand that the game must be played "for the good of the team." The players must also realize that it is a combination of touch and angles, along with consistency, that produces the best results in doubles. Powerful hits and brilliant winner attempts should be saved for the singles court.

In a game of doubles, quicker exchanges of the ball occur as players at the net volley the ball back to the opponents much sooner than would normally occur in singles. This makes for more intense, exciting play. Players also move differently in doubles. Singles play requires more lateral movement, while doubles players move more forward and backward. Good doubles play is *at the net* and since a partner is sharing half the court, less lateral movement is required. Players move *together* in doubles. This helps to offer a shield of defense and to close off any gaping holes for opponents to hit into. It also offers a "balance" so that each team is ideally positioned to cover all balls on each side of the court.

Singles players have difficulty sharing the court and the responsibility for doubles play. To truly become a doubles player though, you must realize that you will *win or lose as a team* and you must be prepared to share the credit or blame with your partner. If you can learn to work together with another, and understand

and play the game as the separate game that it is, you will probably have much success and fun playing the game of doubles.

FINDING THE RIGHT PARTNER

When searching for a partner, look for someone whom you could be a "team player" with. It might be a friend you already have. The important thing is that it should be someone you are compatible with, get along with, and can talk to easily. It's not necessary that the person plays the game in a similar style, although similar levels of players often prove best. You should look for someone who is both *complementary* and *complimentary*.

Flashy players don't make the best partners since the game of doubles is best played with placement, finesse, and percentage stroke-making. It will also be important that you share mutual respect and confidence with your partner to score well with another.

Know which side of the court (forehand/right/deuce or backhand/left/ad) you prefer to play and look for a partner who plays the other side well. The great teams throughout history have had the power player on the left or ad side, with the finesse or steady player on the right side. The consistent player on the right will be able to put more balls into play, giving the team the opportunity to always remain in the lead. The player on the ad side will be the put-a-way partner who can capitalize on the situation created and win the big points. If you're an "ad court" type of player (power, bigger hitter), stay away from pairing up with another player with a similar game style unless you want inconsistent results. On the other hand, if you're a steady player who prefers the deuce court and you choose a partner who also lacks a "knock-out punch," you might find the team is unable to end any of the point. Search

for the partner who will complement your game and help to unify the team's effort.

The last thing you want to feel is embarrassment or guilt after missing each shot. Your partner, and the relationship that you have, will either make you feel that way or not. It will take a mutually supportive balance to keep the team feeling confident. To build a bond of respect, look for a partner who is supportive, forgiving, and sensitive enough to be understanding.

Two right-handed players usually find they work best with the better forehand player on the right side and the player with the better backhand on the left. Left-handers are generally best positioned in the ad side of the court because their backhands appear almost hidden, making it difficult for servers to find. Although these are general guidelines for team formations, each team is unique and should be analyzed to discover each player's strengths, weaknesses, and styles of play. This will help to determine where each should be positioned for the good of the team.

DEVELOPING AS A TEAM

In doubles, it is essential that two heads come together. Without a "meeting of the minds," players may plan and play independently of one another. Shot selections, strategies, and tactical planning can only be shared and decided on as a team. Any other way would simply be playing doubled-up singles!

When two people learn to come together and share what each person sees, hears, feels, and thinks, the overall awareness of the team becomes sharper. When both players turn "on" their computer-minds and unify their mental efforts, each is able to discover and perceive more, and the team benefits as a whole.

Playing as a team requires an implicit understanding of who will take and play each shot on your side of the net. Two common in-decisive situations occur when shots are directed between the two of you down the center of the court and when the ball is played over your head or your partner's head. Which player is closest to the ball in question? The player *closest to the ball* should always be given the right of way. Balls hit down the center are generally played by the better player or better stroke of the two. Balls lobbed up overhead are normally played by the person whose head the ball is going over.

When covering lobs, problems occur when players neglect to communicate their intentions. All balls lobbed up overhead to your side of the court should quickly be called out loud with either a "Mine!" or "Yours!" command. It is imperative that this be stated immediately, without hesitation.

"Let it bounce!" and "Switch!" are two additional commands that can help the team. "Let it bounce" is quickly called by an alert partner to his or her teammate who is about to strike a ball that appears to be traveling out of bounds. "Switch" is stated when one player has crossed over into the same side with his or her partner, and the other player needs to move over to cover the court left vacant.

Once you understand your own games, have taken into account the games of your opponents, and have come together and communicated a strategy, it will then be important to carry out the mission as *one*. Playing as one is the very basis for a solid game of doubles. In other sports, it is common for players to work together. In baseball, the pitcher and catcher become a unit; in football, it's the quarterback and center (and receiver or runner); and in basketball, it's the shooter and assistman or passer. In doubles play, the serving pair must work together to hold serve. The net partner poaches more, or moves across the net to take more balls. The server places the ball with the service delivery for the net person to score success for the team. The receiving team must work even harder to break their opponents' serve. The receiver attempts on the return to place the ball so that the serving team is put on the defensive. Then the net partner can move in to intercept the ball and steal away the offensive.

It is important to always keep in mind that you are not playing against your partner. Everyone has good and bad days so you should be understanding and compassionate with your partner when his game is off, just like you'd like to be treated in return on your bad performance days. Since neither of you can win without the other, learn to bring out the best in your partner by showing the respect, confidence, and support you crave as well.

POSITIONING YOURSELVES FOR SUCCESS

Doubles is a game that is usually best played at the *net*. The team at the net has the advantage, since they are able to "spike" the ball down from this position, similar to the game of volleyball. Seventy percent of all errors in tennis are balls hit into the net. When players stand in close and take balls above the net level they've lowered the risk of netting their shots.

At the highest level of tennis, all four players move towards the net with the winning point typically going to the team who arrived there first. To gain control of the court, start by getting to the net more often. If you're not comfortable with your volley and overhead, start practicing coming in more often. You will both eventually need to learn to *like* to play the net to score your team future success.

An attacking game of doubles brings with it an intimidation factor. Pressure is applied to your opponents, who must attempt to pass you

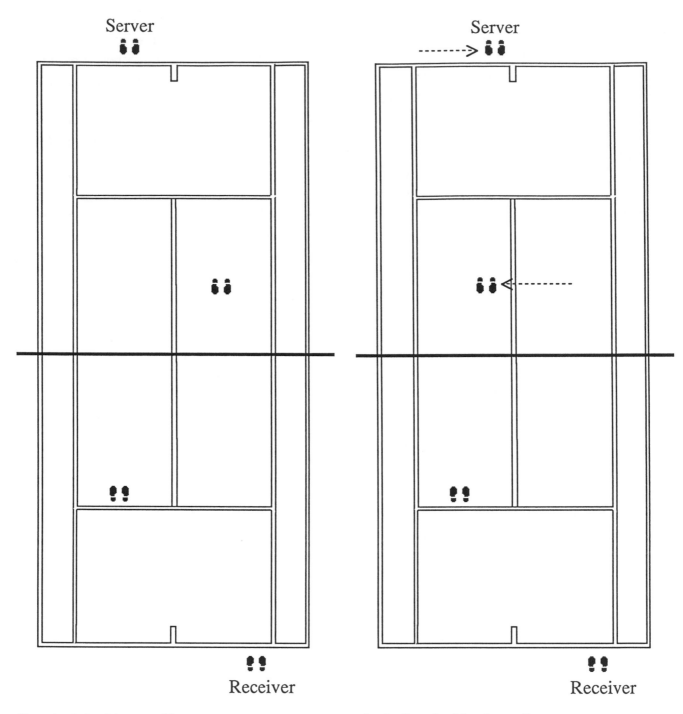

Standard doubles positions.   Australian doubles formation.

or accurately place the ball over your head. This creates a challenge for your opponents that makes many players uncomfortable.

The best doubles teams learn to *move together*. When one shifts out wide, the other shifts an equal distance towards the center. It's as if a rope was tied between the two. When one moves forward, so does the other. When one player moves backward, so does the partner. This way they are balancing the court and playing as one.

Teams who work towards playing *parallel* to one another are stronger than those who remain in the one up/one back formation. Since there is a huge diagonal area left open on the staggered position, opposing teams are able to take advantage by angling shots between them much easier.

One of the most common mistakes in doubles is for players to assume the same positions on court each time they play. The positions in doubles should vary with your opponents. There is really no one right position in doubles; the best one can always be found by using your heads! Alter your positions to get the best angles and results possible. Shift forward for aggressiveness or retreat for more defensive tactics. Both can play back on the baseline if necessary, and partners can even change from the left to the right side of the court to receive serves differently at the end of each set.

You can be creative in your doubles positioning by using a formation called *Australian doubles*. The server stands closer to the center service mark behind the baseline, while the partner shifts to stand in the opposite service box than is customary. With this new formation, the crosscourt shot is taken away as opponents are forced to make the more difficult down-the-line return. You can control the match by switching back and forth between the regular and Australian position until your opponents are completely uncomfortable with

their play. Be learning to experiment a little, you might discover more success through your team's own creativity.

COMMUNICATION MAKES THE DIFFERENCE

A common understanding is needed between two for teamwork to come together. Communication, both verbal and non-verbal, allows the partners to share and discuss strategies and keep the motivation riding high in each, as well as help the team to play better as one.

Silence is a form of communication. If everything is going well for you and your partner and your team is on the winning track, the best communication may be to remain quiet and simply continue playing the same way. Often the most important form of communication you will share with your partner (as well as your opponents) is the expression on your face. A smile or calm look on your face expresses confidence and can relax your partner more than most words.

Whether you are the established leader or follower of your team, being a good communicator requires a talent for *listening*. When you talk less, you learn more! When your partner does talk, listen and learn. It's not always what you say when communicating that is important, but how you say it. You never want to get your partner mad or upset. Try to win her over to your side with tact and finesse. Since communicating is a two-way street, it will be important that you always recognize your partner's feelings when interacting.

Teams often meet on court for brief, in-between-point discussions. What are they talking about? Well . . . they might be sharing what shots they are about to play or where the next ball should be directed. They might be discussing ways to improve team planning and

Through effective conversation players learn to work together as one in the game of doubles.

positioning or they might be talking about something noted with the opposing team. Maybe one of the teammates has fallen off the strategic track and needs to rally back for the team effort . . . or maybe all is well and the players just want to continue "pumping themselves up" to remain keen, intense, and on top!

Communication is a personal thing. You and your partner must decide just how much communication is necessary for your team. You might find it best to keep your on-court talk to a minimum. As with most relationships, however, doubles teams have a history of falling apart when a lack of communication is present.

If you must give advice during your talks make it helpful, not analytical or judgmental. When calling attention to a mistake, use the indirect route to avoid resentment. You can bring out the best or worst in your partner, depending on the effectiveness of your com-

munication skills.

Good partners are good communicators. They are able to talk out their concerns effectively and listen sympathetically when the other has an idea to share. They don't try to change their partner as much as understand and get along with them. They attempt to keep the game positive with themselves and their partner. In the process, they have fewer on-court problems and are the ones who usually score more on-court successes.

DOUBLES STRATEGIES AND TACTICS

The teams who learn to play the *percentages* in doubles have the most favorable odds to perform consistently well.

Doubles is not a game of power but of intelligent use of speed. When players attempt to hit "home runs" on every hit, they will often find themselves making lots of errors in the process. The legendary home-run hitter, Babe Ruth, also held the strike-out record! What does this say of his consistency? Singles players can be the lone star who plays the game this way, but not doubles players. They must learn to become *boring champions*.

Listed below are some basic principles for sound doubles play:

1. The Better Server Serves First. The better server allows your team to get a good start and help the team pull through if the set gets close.

2. Get a High Percentage of First Serves In. Many more points are won when first serves are in. It also keeps the pressure on your opponents and off yourselves.

3. Serve the Ball Down the Middle of the Court. This will limit the angles your opponent can return the serve with and keeps more balls in the center of the court (which allows your partner easier volleys).

4. Hold Serve! If your team doesn't lose its serve, you can't lose the match! The strategy the pros use.

5. Make Consistent Returns. Treat return of serves like second serves. Use care to get all returns into play.

6. Keep the Ball in the Middle of the Court. The net is lower in the center and the angle is taken away for your opponents to pass you from there.

7. Lob if in Doubt. The lob helps eliminate your team's errors, and it can also be your best defense against aggressive play.

8. Take Over the Net. The team who takes over the net has the advantage and the control.

9. The Team with the Fewest Errors Wins! It's not winners who win matches, it's error-free play.

10. Change a Losing Game and Never Change One That's Winning. Learn to change your game as necessary.

Teams who have developed a wide array of strategic plans have increased their chance of success. By learning a lobbing game, an attack game, a patient game, and a consistent game, teams are best prepared for these demands when they occur. When teams are able to play back for defensive maneuvers, play up to the net for offensive plays, and adjust for creating new positions such as Australian doubles formations, they are adaptable for strategic changes. And when they have advanced their shot-making ability to direct the ball both deep and short, high or low and can hit equally well hard or soft, they are best prepared to place the ball effectively during a wide variety of match situations.

The next time you're out playing doubles, slow down and relax. Don't rush about the court. Plan your strokes by allowing a comfortable margin for error on each and then execute them smoothly and safely. Your ability and your partner's ability to reduce errors and make boring shots regularly will be what makes you into champions. You may not look like the flashy singles stars, but you'll be winning matches consistently by your wits, not your appearance.

SUMMARY

To play doubles well, you must first understand that doubles is not singles. When searching for another player to pair with, look for someone who is both complementary and complimentary. You will build a bond of mutual respect with your partner, so search for a supportive, forgiving individual who is sensitive enough to be understanding as well as a good tennis player.

In doubles, the team learns to play as one. Players who play independently of one another are really just playing doubled-up singles. The best teams move together and position themselves at the net for success. They realize that the team at the net has the advantage and control of the point. They also communicate with each other. They talk out their concerns effectively and listen sympathetically when the other has an idea to share. The best teams also perform consistently well because they understand and play the percentages. In the process, they have reduced their errors and have become boring champions.

Appendix

PLAYER DEVELOPMENT: PROGRAM REPORTS & RECORDS

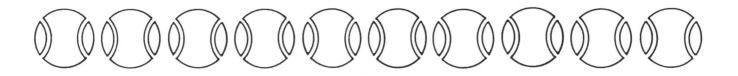

MY TENNIS GOALS

(Date: _____)

SHORT-TERM (3 months-1 year)

Action Steps:

MID-TERM (1-2 years)

Action Steps:

LONG-TERM (2+ years)

Action Steps:

TRAINING SCHEDULE

1. PREPARATION PHASE (5-6 weeks):
Build strength and endurance, drilling, technical and tactical game development, and cross training.

(Dates: _____)

WEEK 1
MON:
TUES:
WED:
THURS:
FRI:
SAT:
SUN:
WEEK 2
MON:
TUES:
WED:
THURS:
FRI:
SAT:
SUN:
WEEK 3
MON:
TUES:
WED:
THURS:
FRI:
SAT:
SUN:

WEEK 4
MON:
TUES:
WED:
THURS:
FRI:
SAT:
SUN:
WEEK 5
MON:
TUES:
WED:
THURS:
FRI:
SAT:
SUN:
WEEK 6
MON:
TUES:
WED:
THURS:
FRI:
SAT:
SUN:
NOTES:

TRAINING SCHEDULE

2. PRE-COMPETITIVE PHASE (3-5 weeks):
Simulate competitive play and higher intensity drills.

(Dates: _____)

WEEK 1
MON:
TUES:
WED:
THURS:
FRI:
SAT:
SUN:
WEEK 2
MON:
TUES:
WED:
THURS:
FRI:
SAT:
SUN:
WEEK 3
MON:
TUES:
WED:
THURS:
FRI:
SAT:
SUN:

WEEK 4
MON:
TUES:
WED:
THURS:
FRI:
SAT:
SUN:

WEEK 5
MON:
TUES:
WED:
THURS:
FRI:
SAT:
SUN:

NOTES:

TRAINING SCHEDULE

3. COMPETITIVE PHASE (2-3 weeks):
Maintain peak performance, increase intensity, lower volume of workouts, tennis specific with reduced off-court activity.

(Dates: _____)

WEEK 1
MON:
TUES:
WED:
THURS:
FRI:
SAT:
SUN:

WEEK 2
MON:
TUES:
WED:
THURS:
FRI:
SAT:
SUN:

WEEK 3
MON:
TUES:
WED:
THURS:
FRI:
SAT:
SUN:

TRAINING SCHEDULE

4. ACTIVE REST PHASE (1-3 weeks):
Break from tennis but maintain level of fitness with cross-training.

(Dates: _____)

WEEK 1	
MON:	
TUES:	
WED:	
THURS:	
FRI:	
SAT:	
SUN:	

WEEK 2	
MON:	
TUES:	
WED:	
THURS:	
FRI:	
SAT:	
SUN:	

WEEK 3	
MON:	
TUES:	
WED:	
THURS:	
FRI:	
SAT:	
SUN:	

LESSON NOTES

LESSON (Date:_____**)**

Things we worked on:

Points to remember:

Homework:

LESSON (Date:_____**)**

Things we worked on:

Points to remember:

Homework:

LESSON (Date:_____**)**

Things we worked on:

Points to remember:

Homework:

PRACTICE PARTNERS/TENNIS BUDDIES LIST

NAME	PHONE	LEVEL
1. _____	_____	_____
2. _____	_____	_____
3. _____	_____	_____
4. _____	_____	_____
5. _____	_____	_____
6. _____	_____	_____
7. _____	_____	_____
8. _____	_____	_____
9. _____	_____	_____
10. _____	_____	_____
11. _____	_____	_____
12. _____	_____	_____

LADDER RESULTS/TOURNAMENT RECORD

Date	Ladder/Tournament	Wins Over	Losses To	Round	Score

PLAYER DEVELOPMENT

Coach's, Parent's, and Player's Report

(Date: _____)

Review for _____ for the period _____

COACH'S COMMENTS:

PARENT'S COMMENTS:

PLAYER'S COMMENTS:

OPPONENT ANALYSIS FORM

NAME: _____ OPPONENT: _____

TOURNAMENT:_____ DATE: _____

WON/LOST: _____ ROUND:_____ SCORE: _____

Did he/she prefer to play on the baseline, rush the net, or mix it up? _____

Would you say he/she's an offensive player, a defensive player, or mixture? _____

Does he/she hit with topspin, underspin, flat, or mixture? _____

Is he/she a patient player or a big hitter? _____

How does he/she handle and react to pressure? _____

Does he/she prefer high or low balls? _____

Does he/she prefer hard or soft balls? _____

Does he/she prefer flat or spin shots? _____

What is his/her favorite shot? _____

What are some of his/her weak strokes? _____

Were you able to play to them? Why or why not? _____

OPPONENT ANALYSIS FORM
(cont.)

Do his/her service returns float high, stay low, play down the middle, or angle wide? _____
_____
_____

How does he/she move (quick, slow, etc.)? _____
_____

Is he/she in shape to last a long match? _____
_____

What shots did he/she hurt you with? _____
_____
_____

What shots did you hurt him/her with? _____
_____
_____

Is he/she a slow starter or a faster starter? _____
_____

Does he/she play better when he's/she's ahead or behind? _____
_____
_____

Was he/she mentally tough? _____
_____

What does he/she tend to do on important points? _____
_____

Is he/she beatable? Why or why not? _____
_____
_____
_____

How I will play and beat him/her in our next meeting: _____
_____
_____

MATCH CRITIQUE SHEET

NAME:_____ DATE: _____

TOURNAMENT: _____ OPPONENT: _____

WON/LOST: _____ ROUND:_____ SCORE: _____

PLAY:	Excellent	Good	Fair	Poor
Concentration	_____	_____	_____	_____
Hustle	_____	_____	_____	_____
Attitude	_____	_____	_____	_____
Strategy	_____	_____	_____	_____
Sportsmanship	_____	_____	_____	_____
STROKES:				
Forehand	_____	_____	_____	_____
Backhand	_____	_____	_____	_____
Volley	_____	_____	_____	_____
Serve	_____	_____	_____	_____
Return of Serve	_____	_____	_____	_____
Overhead	_____	_____	_____	_____
Drop Shot	_____	_____	_____	_____
Approach Shot	_____	_____	_____	_____
Other_____	_____	_____	_____	_____

Your strengths in the match were:

You could use improvement in these areas:

Your own comments on the match:

INDIVIDUAL EVALUATION CHART

NAME:_____ DATE: _____

TOURNAMENT: _____ OPPONENT: _____

WON/LOST: _____ ROUND:_____ SCORE: _____

COMMENTS: _____

SYMBOLS

cc =	crosscourt	F =	Forehand	AS =	Approach Shot
dl =	down-the-line	B =	Backhand	DS =	Drop Shot
w =	wide	L =	Lob	OH =	Overhead
l =	long	V =	Volley	SR =	Service Return
n =	netted	HV =	Half Volley	DF =	Double Fault
				SW =	Serve Winner

1st SET			2nd SET			3rd SET		
SERVICE	POINTS	ERRORS	SERVICE	POINTS	ERRORS	SERVICE	POINTS	ERRORS

"Special" For Readers of the *Junior Tennis Handbook*:

Skip Singleton's Intelligent Tennis T-Shirt/Sweatshirt

Adult T-Shirt (100% cotton) Reg. $15.00 **Special price** $12.95
Adult Sweatshirt (50/50) Reg. $25.00 **Special price** $22.95
Children's T-Shirt (50/50) Reg. $12.00 **Special price** $10.95

Shirts are white, quality 100% cotton or cotton/poly and are screen printed with puffed neon balls in the same design as the cover of this book.

Adult Sizes—S, M, L, XL
Children Sizes—XS (2-4), S (6-8), M (10-12), L (14-16)

To order, send check or money order for total amount for shirt(s) plus $3.00 for shipping and handling. (Make check payable to "Intelligent Tennis Shirts".) Please be sure to indicate: style(s) (t-shirt or sweatshirt) and size(s) when ordering.

SEND ORDERS TO:

Skip Singleton's Intelligent Tennis Shirts
P.O. Box 5021
Niceville, FL 32578

ABOUT THE AUTHOR

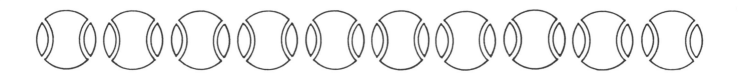

Skip Singleton has received the distinct honor of being named a USPTA Master Professional, one of only 70 USPTA Master Professionals in the world and the youngest Master Pro ever at age 31. He has authored two other popular books, *Intelligent Tennis* and *Intelligent Doubles*, both published by Betterway Publications. Skip is the Director of Tennis at Bluewater Bay Resort in Niceville, Florida. Bluewater Bay was selected by *Tennis Magazine* as "One of the Top 50 Greatest U.S. Tennis Resorts" and *World Tennis Magazine* named Bluewater Bay to its "Top 25 Resorts" list while giving it a 5-Star Rating. The Florida Tennis Association also named Bluewater Bay its "Tennis Club of the Year" 1986-87 and 1988-89, the only club ever to receive this distinct honor twice. Skip was named "Professional of the Year" by the USPTA Florida Division for 1989. He has held state and national rankings since he was a junior and has competed on professional circuits throughout the U.S. and Europe. He has worked both on and off the court with internationally known and respected coaches and players and has served the tennis industry in a wide variety of capacities. Skip is an active speaker nationally and is a member of the Prince Professional Advisory Staff. He lives with his wife, Debbie, and dogs Ace and Volley in Bluewater Bay Resort in Niceville, Florida.

INDEX

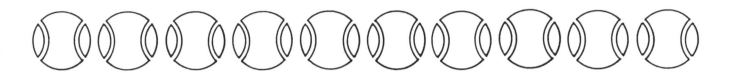